The Successful Student

How to Develop Good Study Habits

Patricia Orlunwo Ikiriko

The Successful Student

First published in 2013 by

Panoma Press

48 St Vincent Drive, St Albans, Herts, AL1 5SJ, UK

info@panomapress.com

www.panomapress.com

Book layout by Charlotte Mouncey

Printed on acid-free paper from managed forests.

ISBN 978-1-909623-18-7

The right of Patricia Orlunwo Ikiriko to be identified as the author of this work has been asserted in accordance with sections 77 and 78 of the Copyright Designs and Patents Act 1988.

A CIP catalogue record for this book is available from the British Library.

This book is available online and in bookstores.

Praise for the book

Patricia Ikiriko does a thorough job in explaining clearly from first principles how to get into the right frame of mind for studying and the practical steps one should take to achieve one's goals, including tips about time management, self-belief, self-responsibility and learning styles.

Catherine O'Brien PhD
Cambridge University UK

I believe strongly that this book will mark a change in many lives.

Mrs Iberie Addey , Senior Business Consultant, International Business Machines Corporation, IBM United Kingdom (UK)

This book is primarily a study guide aimed at undergraduate students, students aspiring to gain admission into the tertiary institutions, and every major stakeholder who has vested interest in improving the academic achievement of the present generation.

It provides basic insight on some hidden psychological factors such as fear, anxiety, low self-esteem, poor self-efficacy and external locus of control which militate against students' academic achievement and proffers realistic techniques such as

SMARTS, BREAKS, and ACADEMIC SUCCESS TIPS among others as relevant solutions to combat these psychological maladies.

Decision + Determination + Hard work = Distinction, is a great formulae of success to internalize.

Dr Chinelo Ugwu , Counselling Psychologist, University of Port Harcourt, Nigeria

I found this book very interesting, up to date and informative. It is very beneficial especially for all formal learners and teachers in a learning process and career planning. It discusses internal and external factors that affect a learning process and their solution. It also develops confidence in students to achieve their goals. At least it encourages me in my studies.

Sadia Aleem, University of Bedfordshire, Department of Psychology Research Student, LU1 3JU, UK

This book is a "must-read" for everyone desiring to be successful at whatever they choose to do - (be it learning, studying or accomplishing any given tasks) because of the practical tips and life changing techniques it provides at every chapter.

Eric I. Ekwe, BSc (Hons); MBA; PGD; MSc - Tech Mgmt. CASSIDIAN.

So many things I thought 'I cannot do' become 'things I might be able to do'. I believe that taking responsibility for your learning, after reading this wonderful book, cannot be very difficult anymore!! This book provided necessary background information and offered solutions to replace bad study habits and apply the new one to the real world. Only six steps between moving from your drawbacks old habits to the outstanding new habits ... Find them now inside this book!!

Saleh Alkhathami,
University of Bedfordshire
Department of Psychology Research Student

This book is an invaluable aid because it is simple, easy to read and practical. It tells you not only 'what' to do but 'how' to excel as a student.

Gbenga Apampa
Vice President (Sustainable Development)
TOTAL Head Office. Paris. France

Dedication

This book is dedicated to my loving and caring husband Hon (Evang) Hope Odhuluma Ikiriko, My late father chief Mark Addey and my lovely mother Mrs Agnes Addey, my late parent's in-law Rev & Mrs Howard Ikiriko, my loving children Doxa Chiudushime and Chanan-Christie, and my little granddaughter Sarah-Louisa Seker. Hon. (Barr.) Ezebunwo Nyesom Wike. The Honorable Minister of State for Education in Nigeria. For his relentless effort in transforming the education sector under his watch.

Acknowledgments

I am grateful to many people for their support and kind help in writing this book.

First, my husband Hon (Evang) Hope Odhuluma Ikiriko for his endless love; always being there to help support me morally and financially throughout the endeavour. To my lovely mother Mrs Agnes Addey for her love and tender care, counsel, prayers and always been there for me.

Dr Joseph Adonu, for his encouragement and mentoring. Despite his busy schedule, he always found time to provide guidance in a timely manner.

Professor Andrew Guppy for being supportive, providing useful materials, and spurring me on to aspire higher in my academic journey.

To my little children Doxa and Chanan who have given their love and encouragement as I shared my attention between them and this work.

Also to Tracey Dixon and Patricia-Lynn Dixon for their patience in proofreading every part of this book and to Mrs Grace Dixon for her tireless moral support. To my sister in-law Dr Mrs Patricia Ogbonaya for her love.

To my wonderful PhD colleagues Andrew Clements, Fatahyah Yahya, Saleh Alkhathami, Anatoli Karypidou, and Sarah Baker, who have supported me immensely throughout our journey together.

Hon (Barr) Ezebunwo Nyesom Wike for his moral and financial support.

To my dear friend Mrs Bunmi Apampa, my lovely sisters Buduka J Addey, Blessing Oldiedie; my brothers Mr & Dr Mrs Godson Addey, Joseph Addey, Mr & Mrs Ukoma Addey, Arthur Addey and my big daughters Naomi Izevbizua, Timi Seker, Ada Ogaree, my son-in law Pierre Seker, and Sokari Ogaree whose encouragement and moral support have been invaluable.

Finally, my gratitude goes to God Almighty, the pillar of my life, for the inspiration and knowledge in completing this unique idea.

Preface

I was an average student who once failed, in Year 10 (equivalent to Senior Secondary 2 in the Nigerian education system). As a young student, I was afraid of learning or attempting to learn anything new. Consequently, this flawed my perception about my ability to perform well in my studies. This in turn led to test anxiety and misconceptions about the possibility of attaining good results in the future.

Effective study habits are a prerequisite for putting students on a path of educational success, but this was an essential aspect that was lacking in my own agenda as a young student. I had no knowledge of how to study, do some reading on topics before the class, take proper notes in class, or carefully review notes after class, no dedicated schedule of study time, and no fixed aims in mind. Although I attended classes, I did not pay proper attention to what was being taught, and failed to prepare adequately for examinations, feeling others were responsible for my poor performance.

In my final year, I made a decision to work hard, and gradually the fear within me and negative attitudes changed towards studying. I identified suitable learning styles, stated objectives, set goals, followed new methods of studying, and maintained a sense of high self-concept. This firm belief in my ability to succeed and determination against all odds let me to achieve my goals. My educational career improved accordingly: for my GCE (equivalent to GCSE), I achieved 4 A stars and 3 B+. My solid performance continued for my first degree, a Master's degree, including my postgraduate diploma in United Kingdom. I am currently in my PhD progression in the UK, adopting the same attitudes.

Decision + Determination + Hardwork = Distinction.

You too can make it!

Contents

Introduction

Learning is, as The Oxford English Dictionary (OED) tells us, 'the acquisition of knowledge or skills through study, experience, or being taught.'

While this is undoubtedly true, this definition neglects to consider the necessity for what we study, experience, or are taught to be committed to memory. Learning has most value when it is embedded, meaning that we are able to call upon the knowledge and/or skills we acquire effortlessly whenever they are needed.

Simply being told something or even experiencing it for ourselves will not automatically result in our subsequently having that information at our fingertips. Learning is actually more complex than that. Learning is active, not passive. And yet despite the many things pupils are taught in schools, the art of conscious and active learning is rarely one of them.

Teachers may manage much of students' learning in that they create lesson plans that adhere to the curriculum and so are designed to give them the knowledge necessary to pass exams. They may also offer guidance as to how to schedule periods of revision prior to those exams, but they generally don't spend time explaining the wide range of issues that can inhibit and impact adversely upon students' academic performance and success.

These include students' learning styles and learning preferences, and how to make useful notes that aid memory as well as recording data, as well as how to undertake active learning. They often don't even teach in a manner that would encourage and enable the process of learning, preferring instead to simply lecture their students; the equivalent of throwing knowledge out and hoping some of it sticks.

Consequently it is clear that learning can be greatly enhanced if students have the ability to manage the process for themselves. To do this, students need to have the ability to manage their time, structure their study periods, break down large tasks into more manageable ones, set achievable goals and objectives, persevere even under difficult circumstances, establish ways in which they may monitor and measure their learning progress, adjust their learning strategies as necessary, and know how they might overcome any difficulties they encounter in the process.

In education, sometimes you may feel afraid that the study task you have at hand is so big that you cannot accomplish it on your own; you shrink from it and feel emotionally battered when you fail. You become increasingly anxious when it comes to learning or trying any new thing. This is a natural human tendency. What you need to do is face up to the challenges, develop the ability to pick yourself up and master the process of simply getting started. Your destination will be reached by a series of small steps, not one giant leap.

Some people are slow learners, some are fast learners, and others are learners who find it very hard to get things done. No matter where you fit, do not worry, but celebrate because you have within yourself all that it takes to succeed. Some simple strategies will help you to change your academic challenges for the better.

Students who leave school with the autonomy to set their own learning goals and with the confidence that they know how to achieve those goals are much better equipped to learn throughout their lives. This is a huge benefit, as learning is a lifelong adventure. Learning might start out as simply needing to know the answers in order to do well in a test or pass an exam, but what it's really about is equipping oneself with the ability to progress and improve continuously throughout life.

Learning is less about the simple acquisition of knowledge and more about questioning, reasoning, understanding and gaining wisdom. *When someone knows how to learn, they become an active controller of their own learning rather than a passive consumer of education.* The emphasis is on personal growth: those who control their own learning have the capacity to get more out of study and more out of life.

Possessing a genuine interest in the subjects being taught and studied in school, college and university is important as well. Students who hold a sincere interest in a subject are likely to be far more motivated to manage their own learning and develop the requisite skills to become effective learners of that subject. Hence we can see that the student's existing level of interest is highly relevant when considering the development of effective learning strategies for any academic subject — or indeed, when choosing what subjects to study in more depth.

In contrast, anxiety about learning can act as a barrier to effective learning. Students who feel anxious about their ability to cope in academic learning situations may seek to actively avoid them and thus be deprived of important career and life opportunities.

By far the majority of students' learning time is spent in formal education, whether school, college or university. This in turn means that the climate and culture of an educational establishment is vitally important for the creation of an effective learning environment.

Culture may be explained as 'the way we do things around here', and the way things are done in an educational establishment should be designed to be as inclusive as possible. Rigid strictures as to what is acceptable or ideal will alienate more students than it embraces, and will ultimately prove harmful. The existence of a culture that welcomes discovery, challenge, and personal development will encourage learning far more effectively than one seeking to impose norms of dress, values and thought. If a student feels alienated and disengaged from the learning contexts in the educational establishment they attend, his or her potential to master fundamental skills and concepts, and develop effective learning skills, is likely to be adversely affected.

Target audience

This book is aimed primarily at students engaged in formal education at tertiary level. It is likely that it will also be of benefit to secondary level pupils, especially those preparing for formal examinations.

In addition, any individual who has an interest in understanding the learning process and utilising that knowledge in order to achieve an educational career, or to develop and progress further in their employment, will find this book useful, as will anyone with the need to acquire a higher level of skill in the art of learning in order to help others (for example, teachers, tutors and trainers).

Parents and guardians of students engaged in formal education will find value in the text. Even government bodies that have a vested interest in the educational development and legal rights of persons in education may find it helpful.

Aims and objectives

It is important to remember that it is not just study techniques that can have a bearing on a student's academic outcome, but that there are hidden psychological factors which must be identified and confronted. Such factors include: fear and anxiety, low self-esteem, poor self-efficacy, external locus of control and a poor self-concept. The aim of the book is to offer genuine and relevant solutions to the hidden psychological fears that prevent students from attempting to actualise their dream. It also considers the learning process and individual learning styles, as well as planning, time management, setting realistic and achievable goals and objectives, staying focused, applying self-motivation strategies, and the different approaches that may be taken to learning. The overall objective is to both encourage and empower students to develop the ability to think freely and rationally; to organise themselves, their time, and their work; and to approach tests and examinations with confidence. To attain this objective, a range of issues must be addressed.

This book will help you to...

- Identify those hidden factors that inhibit your academic performance.

- Build your confidence and discover your potential.

- Get the grades you want in tests and exams.

- Improve or change those aspects of your personal life with which you are unhappy.

- Take a strategic approach to enable you to achieve your goals or ambitions.

- Have more time for the things you value and enjoy about your studies.

- Create, focus on and work towards present and future opportunities, rather than dwell on unsatisfactory past experiences or errors committed in previous examinations.

- Start afresh from today with fresh skills and a new mindset; take it from here and move forward.

- Consider all the options available to you and decide on what actions you want to try out to help you achieve your goals and deal effectively with your academic concerns.

The book is written in straightforward language in order to facilitate the widest possible understanding of the information it contains. As well as offering information, it includes tips, tactics and techniques that may be used to help students increase their level of learning success.

If you are prepared to take what you learn here and put it into practise, you can increase your chances of success, not just for now but for the rest of your life.

Chapter 1: Studying

Studying is related to the acquisition of knowledge. Knowledge is defined by The Oxford English Dictionary (OED) as 'facts, information, and skills acquired through experience or education; the theoretical or practical understanding of a subject'.

If knowledge is measured solely by the output of research papers, then it has grown at a rate of 7.2 per cent per annum in the UK since 2006. That places the UK second only to the US in terms of this measure. World average growth during the period was 6.3 per cent. In order that you can remain effective, whether as a student, an academic, an entrepreneur or an employee, you must be able to keep up with change and with the increased amount of relevant information that will become available to you.

It has been estimated that in 1912, a person might read fifty books in their entire lifetime; nowadays we can be presented with that much information in a day. What you know today is unlikely to be sufficient in a year's time, and may be completely redundant in five years' time.

Consider the following 'facts' that were once known by scientists:

- 6 years ago: Pluto is a planet.

- 100 years ago: the universe is static.

- 130 years ago: the smallest particle is the atom.

- 500 years ago: the Earth is at the centre of the universe.

- 2500 years ago: the Earth is flat.

People who are able to take control of their learning and learn effectively will be at a distinct advantage in a world where things can change both radically and at an alarming rate.

The ideal time to develop good learning habits is as a student; that way, you've got them for life.

The four stages of learning

Whatever it may be that we are studying with a view to learning and acquiring knowledge, there are four stages through which we progress. In sequential order they are:

- unconscious incompetence;

- conscious incompetence;

- conscious competence; and

- unconscious competence.

Let's take a look at each of these in a little more detail.

1. Unconscious incompetence

This is the stage where you don't know how to do something, but aren't yet aware of your lack of knowledge. If you have not previously considered the concept of learning to learn, then you can consider yourself to be at this particular stage. You will not move on until you have acknowledged both the value of the skill and your own incompetence. If you do not value the skill, and so do not care that you lack competence, then there is no reward for learning. The greater the desire and impetus to learn, the less time you will spend in this stage.

As you begin to take charge of and responsibility for your own learning, and start on the path to personal development, you are conscious that you are going to learn something, although not conscious, as yet, of the complexity of your learning goals. To begin to want to learn you must move on to the next stage.

2. Conscious incompetence

Have you learned to drive yet? If so, remember how it felt and the processes you went through. If not, imagine that you are going to learn. You will have been told that you must be able to use the mirrors, the indicators, the pedals, the gears and so on, and to be cognisant of the highway code. As daunting as it may feel, you have an initial understanding of the complexity of your learning goal.

Whatever you are learning will require you to:

- adopt new behaviours and attitudes;

- break down complex tasks into smaller steps;

- make progress one step at a time;

- accept and learn from criticism;

- take responsibility for the situation and the outcome — only you can make sure that you succeed; and,

- face up to whatever problems arise and work hard to overcome them.

Because you are aware of the complexity of your learning goal and are working steadily towards competence, you are conscious of your own current incompetence; this is the 'clumsy' stage of development.

3. Conscious competence

You've now mastered the skill of driving with sufficient competence to pass your driving test. Well done! But although you have demonstrated to an examiner that you are able to drive, and proved that your skills are up to scratch, you still have to concentrate when you are behind the wheel because your driving skills are new; they have not yet become 'second nature'. In other words, you are consciously competent.

4. Unconscious competence

Over time and with use and practise, your skills become second nature; you drive to college or into town and only remember the journey if something unusual happens and you are required to react in some way. The rest of the time you operate on autopilot; you are not driving carelessly or dangerously, but with skills that are so ingrained you are able to call upon them unconsciously.

And so it is with learning. Applying yourself to the process of learning how to learn now will pay dividends in the future as you call upon those skills both unconsciously and naturally for the rest of your life.

Studying habits in context

Many students enter tertiary education without realising that they must improve their ability and academic capability on all fronts. You are unlikely to be spoon-fed information at this level, but will need to learn to seek out information and think for yourself. The more you are unfamiliar with the subject matter, the more difficult it will be to remember details about a particular topic during tests or examinations. This will hinder class assessment

and make your homework more difficult. The more time you devote to activities other than studying, the more difficult it will be when you start sitting examinations or undergoing any other form of assessment.

How studying differs from reading

One of the first things you'll discover as a student is that studying academic work is different from simply reading a text. While a lot of what you were taught in your early years is likely to remain useful to you, as you advance academically you will want to understand things clearly, develop an in-depth knowledge of the subject(s) you study, and express concepts and ideas in your own words, coherently and concisely. As you gain more knowledge, you will find many new topics interesting and often spend extra time trying to obtain more information about them.

When it comes to reading, it ought to be safe to assume that students have sufficient mastery of the skill to be considered 'unconsciously competent'. But is that enough for study?

(We will return to this subject and examine it in more depth in Chapter 7 'The best way to read a book')

Concept of study habits

Exactly how does a student make a successful transition from just reading to actively studying?

The first thing that you will need to understand is how to develop good 'study habits'. While study habits might be defined in many ways, there are three concepts that you need to understand before you achieve academic success.

Study habits refer to a way of maintaining **a dedicated study schedule** and ensuring uninterrupted time for studying and learning in order that you may **achieve the aims of studying**. When you read, you skim the surface, but when you study, you **discover the treasure within the context** of the words.

So the three key concepts may be re-stated as follows:

1. Devise and stick to a dedicated study schedule.

2. Set and strive to achieve goals and objectives.

3. As you acquire knowledge, seek to discover the deeper meaning inherent in the words you read.

If this is not how you currently apply yourself to studying and learning, that's fine; you are now 'consciously incompetent' as far as that goes, and a great deal of the information contained in the rest of this book will be directly relevant to you in your quest to develop good study habits and to make them second nature.

In the short term, you may feel that you are adding to an already substantial burden by deciding to develop new study habits in addition to acquiring all of the new knowledge you need to take on board in order that you may be successful, but trust me: the time you invest in learning these new habits now will be paid back to you in spades once you've got the habit.

Basic facts you need to remember

You are not a failure. Far from it. If you are at university or college, then you have already enjoyed considerable success when it comes to studying and learning. However, you can use the talent, time and opportunities available to you to consistently work productively and achieve meaningful set objectives.

There are some basic but key study habits that need to be mastered, but you have all it takes to get to the top. Bear in mind that the most prominent professors and award winners were not geniuses. Goertzel and Goertzel (1962) and Goertzel and Hanson (2004)) carried out research and found that three out of five eminent people, including Nobel Prize winners, suffered from academic problems. What made them different was that they did something positive that changed their lives by reinventing themselves or devising a game plan that would enable them to get what they desired in life. Call it whatever you like; as long as you take it seriously and put it into practice; you are creating one of the basic principles of productivity.

Seven decisions that will determine your educational success

Your decision to...

1. Develop a goal for your studies.

2. Excel in your educational career.

3. Follow your study schedule with expectations of a specific result.

4. Honour your teachers' and tutors' instructions.

5. Follow in the footsteps of successful students.

6. Search out the best method of study for you.

7. Conquer procrastination and fear.

Remember: When you read, you skim the surface, but when you study, you discover the treasure within.

Exercise

Think about how you currently apply yourself to studying. What are your habits? How successful are they? With regard to your current ability to study productively and learn actively, where do you currently sit with regard to the four stages of learning that we discussed above?

Be honest when you make this assessment because the rest of the book is going to explain to you in straightforward and practical terms how you can improve at the skill of learning. An accurate assessment now will enable you to see just how far you have progressed in, say, three months' time.

Be prepared to reassess your current level of competence as you learn more about what is involved in developing good study habits. Perhaps you will find that you were more competent than you originally thought — or perhaps you will find that you initially overestimated your ability. Again, be honest. This is all about personal development, and so it is all to your advantage. If you have to develop an attitude of "I CAN" when starting a project then you are more likely to succeed.

List three basic steps that you would take in order to start the project at hand now.

Chapter 2: Understanding student attitudes

You might think that the opportunity to study what you like and how you like would be sufficient to ensure that you approached the task with enthusiasm and a genuine hunger for knowledge, but this is often not the case. When someone appears to be unprepared to take full advantage of a situation, we might say that they don't have the right attitude. An attitude refers to an individual's way of thinking or feeling about things. It is a complex reaction to many factors including experience and expectation. If you have experienced failure at a certain subject in the past, you may expect to fail in the future and, because of this negative attitude, you may well fail. Similarly, if you never expect to be in the top ten per cent of students, it is unlikely that you will be.

Happily attitudes are not set in stone. Some might be harder to change than others, but with the right techniques and some hard work and commitment, it is possible to become who you want to be, rather than who you might believe yourself to be now.

Your attitudes determine your altitude!

Locus of control

American psychologist Julian B. Rotter (1954) was working in the field of personality psychology when he devised a theory which described a unique understanding of the ways in which people believe they can influence events and outcomes in their lives. He termed this 'locus of control', or LOC, and explained it as follows.

A person who believes they are in control of their own life is said to have an internal LOC ('locus' simply means 'location'). In contrast, a person who believes that they have no influence over what happens to them is said to have an external LOC.

Rotter's conceptualises locus of control as uni-dimensional characteristic in that it is either internal or external. Moreover, he equated internal with 'good' and external with 'bad'.

Individuals with an internal locus of control believe that they have the power to influence their own life situations and take responsibility when they fail.

Individuals with an external locus of control attribute the causes of events to external forces, such as other people or organisations who hold a position of power (termed 'powerful others'), fate, chance, and environmental factors.

Park and Kim (1998) contend that people who have an external LOC tend to be unaware of their own negative attitudes and outcomes, preferring to believe that their rewards and punishments are always the result of external forces.

Relating LOC to student experiences

Students who believe that the results of their examinations are due to their own effort and ability are said to have an internal LOC; whereas those who believe that their grades are caused by powerful others, bad luck, the test structure, or the faults of the teacher are said to have an external LOC.

This illustrates how it is that an external LOC is perceived to be negative when compared to an internal LOC viewpoint. The latter perspective is about accepting responsibility for both actions and the outcomes of our action. These individuals tend to have a good *self-concept* and high *self-efficacy*. In contrast, those individuals with an external LOC tend to have a poor *self-concept* and low *self-efficacy*.

Self-concept is related to, but arguably more complex than, self-esteem. While self-esteem may be thought of as having a sense of self-respect and an inherent confidence in one's own worth or abilities, self-concept incorporates the reactions of others to oneself. Your self-concept can be shaped and altered, becoming an amalgamation of your own beliefs about who and how you are, and the reactions you provoke and observe in others.

Self-efficacy is related to competence and is specifically related to an individual's abilities. One can be said to have low self-efficacy if one perceives oneself as incompetent to achieve anything good. Students who believe they are incapable of achieving good results because of their own efforts are less likely to try to improve their academic performance. They are more likely to blame others, to attribute their failure to circumstances, and to avoid taking personal responsibility for the outcome.

It has been argued that LOC is one of the most influential factors related to poor study habits and academic performance Rotter stressed that a state of internal or external LOC was an extreme. Each represents either end of a continuum, with people operating at different points along the continuum at different times and in different circumstances or for different tasks.

It is accepted that, as well as internal and external LOC, there is a third state, termed bi-local. This comprises a mix of the other two states. So, for example, a bi-local student may accept that it is his or her responsibility to study (internal LOC) but accept the need for assistance from powerful others — experts or academics — in order to fully realise his or her potential (external LOC).

Two powerful influences on student behaviours are attitudes and habits, discussed in more detail next.

Attitudes

Attitude is a way of feeling, thinking, beliefs or opinion held that influence a person action and behaviour. Attitude refers to the favourable or unfavourable evaluation of individuals, objects, events, ideas, or indeed anything about which you might form an opinion (Eagly & Chaiken, 1998). Ambivalence is also a recognised state, where someone might have mixed feelings about something.

Many other experts assert that the majority of attitudes you hold are the result of conditioning or social learning, (learning from the environment you find yourself) and as such, attitudes can change with experience.

Habits

The Oxford English Dictionary (OED) tells us that a habit is: 'a settled or regular tendency or practice, especially one that is hard to give up'. Habit is closely related to self-image. We hand in a piece of work late or allow friends to interrupt us when we'd planned to study because that's just the way things always happen to us, even though we swore we'd never allow it to happen again.

Luckily, habits can be changed and 'bad' or self-destructive ones can be replaced by new and more positive ones, but it takes hard work and dedication to make the change, especially since some habits may be so deep-rooted that we're not even aware of them. What we need to do is to identify the bad ones and consciously plan to replace them with better ones.

Simply making a conscious decision that it's time to change a bad habit is a positive move in itself, and once you've taken that first, vital step, then it's time to make a list.

Six positive steps towards breaking a bad habit

Following the steps below will help you to focus your mind on what you are going to do, including why, how and when, in order to replace a bad habit with a better one.

The six steps you should take:

- **Step 1:** Identify and write down your desired new habit. (A positive affirmation of the outcome of change.)

- **Step 2:** State your objective. (Describe how you will behave from now on.)

- **Step 3:** Consider the drawbacks of the old habit. (What are the costs of not changing?)

- **Step 4:** Consider the benefits of the new habit. (What are the rewards for change?)

- **Step 5:** Commit yourself to change. (Accept responsibility and take charge.)

- **Step 6:** Set deadlines for implementing change. (Make sure you can assess and evaluate your progress. and celebrate your success.)

Let's say your bad habit is that you procrastinate, that is, putting off and delaying your studying. Your six-point plan might look similar to the one below.

- **Step 1:** I never put things off just because they might be difficult or unpleasant.

- **Step 2:** As of now, I am going to start my day by doing first the thing I most want to put off.

- **Step 3:** If I put things off I run the risk of missing opportunities or of making potentially difficult situations much worse.

- **Step 4:** If I deal with these things immediately, I don't have them hanging over me and dragging me down.

- **Step 5:** I am going to tell my tutor and my study group about my intentions. By telling them, I am making a commitment to action; I don't want to be seen as someone who cannot be taken seriously.

- **Step 6:** At first, I will deal with difficult or unpleasant things immediately when they arise.

After two weeks, I will prioritise all items on a daily 'to do' list. After one month, I will never again procrastinate.

As you can see, it takes time, commitment and hard work, but bad habits can be changed for the better.

Self-concept

As we discussed above, the term 'self-concept' describes a view of yourself that is a combination of what you know or believe to be true about yourself combined with the reactions of others towards you. This view embraces such elements as beliefs regarding your personality traits, physical characteristics, abilities, and how you experience life.

If your goals of learning to study effectively and working hard to achieve your full potential are to be realised, then it is essential that you protect and maintain a sense of high self-concept and a firm belief in your ability to succeed, no matter what the obstacles.

But how do you stay calm and composed, and maintain a healthy and positive self-concept, when you find yourself in a tough environment?

Protecting your self-concept

There's a danger of getting caught up in a cycle of destructive thinking and behaviour that can sorely damage your self-concept. You may find yourself surrounded by people who are critical of you and who constantly belittle your appearance, taste, personality, dress sense, way of speaking or, indeed, anything else about you.

This kind of situation has the potential to be enormously destructive. If you don't protect yourself against such negativity, then it can have the potential to destroy your sense of self-worth and pull you into the practice of inflicting similar treatment on others. This can happen insidiously: you don't make a conscious decision to change or to begin behaving in a destructive way; you are simply shaped and influenced by what is around you.

So what should you try to avoid, or distance yourself from? Here are some things to think about.

Negative environment: It can be a harsh 'dog eat dog' world, with people fighting just to stay in the same place, never mind get ahead. This is the kind of environment in which brash, aggressive people often thrive. The real danger is that if you are trapped in such an environment, you cannot win, no matter what you do. No one will appreciate your contributions even if you miss lunch and dinner, and stay up late. Often you will fall behind without any chance of getting help from the people around you.

Avoid such situations at all costs: it will ruin your self-concept and damage your sense of self-efficacy. Competition is unavoidable; it is to be found everywhere. Be healthy enough to compete, but only when the situation encourages and rewards healthy competition or if there is a worthwhile value to be won.

Other people's behaviour: You will find that you come up against many different people exhibiting a range of behaviour, not all of them positive. Being faced on a regular basis with negative attitudes and behaviour will threaten both your self-concept and the success of your self-improvement scheme.

Many of these behaviours are the result of people lashing out against what they believe to be an adverse external LOC. Remember that, and preserve your belief in your own capacity and ability to change the world around you by your actions.

Changing environment: The only thing you can guarantee will stay the same is that things will always change. Change is often uncomfortable; it pushes us out of our comfort zone, tests our flexibility and adaptability, and alters the way we think. Learning is all about change: changing habits, changing attitudes and changing opinions. Change will very often make life difficult for a while. It may cause stress, but it will help you find ways to improve three things: 1) our attitude, 2) our behaviour and 3) our way of thinking. Since change is constant we must be open to it.

Failure: It's okay to fail. In fact the only people who don't fail are people who never try to do something new or different. Those people also tend not to grow or develop. Don't allow fear of failure to cause you to be in stasis (a state of stagnation). Treat each failure or error as a learning opportunity and a chance to develop your knowledge and skills.

World view: A world view is a set of assumptions about physical and social reality that may have powerful effects on your thoughts and behaviour. A personal world view is the basic reasoning orientation of an individual which determines their perception and level of understanding.

Develop a vision of what you want to get out of studies and visualise your future career. Look at your study aims and objectives to attain success. Try not to get bogged down with all the negativities of the world. In building self-concept, you must learn how to make the best out of bad situations.

Determination: The way you are and your behavioral traits are said to be a mixed end-product of your inherited genetic traits, your upbringing, and your environmental surroundings such as your parents, school, and circle of friends. You have your own identity. Even if a parent or one or more family members have experienced failure, it doesn't automatically follow that you will be a failure too. Determine and aim to learn from other people's experience, so as to avoid making the same mistakes. Sometimes you may wonder if some people are born leaders or are naturally positive thinkers. NO. Being positive and staying positive is a choice. God isn't going to come down from heaven and tell you 'Patricia, you now have the permission to build your self-concept and improve yourself.' Building your self-concept and drawing lines for self-improvement is a choice, not a rule or a talent.

Anxiety: Poor academic performance is often attributed to high test anxiety. Those students who under-achieve academically tend to have negative beliefs about their ability to do well in their studies. This in turn leads to test anxiety.

The Victorian philosopher William James said: 'There is but one cause of human failure. And that is man's lack of faith in his true self.' It has been found that students who fail their examinations tend to hold misconceptions and negative beliefs about the possibility of attaining good results in the future. This anxiety can have deleterious effects on their academic performance. Poor self-efficacy causes anxiety which can in turn result in a negative self-concept. Try to avoid falling into this vicious circle.

Fear: This is defined here as *False Evidence Appearing Real* (a widely used acronym of unknown origin).

F = False

E = Evidence

A = Appearing

R = Real

Remember that 'impossible' is just a word.

Everyone, at some point in their life, has suffered from the fear of being a failure, somebody who can't make it in life. Who hasn't imagined themselves as the one who will drop out of a game or school? Who hasn't dreaded the unknown? And how many times have you felt anguished at the prospect of being poor, or a failure, or unhappy with your relationships or your grade at school?

Fear is a common problem. Many people get trapped in a cycle of negative thought: *I can't do this. It's too hard. It's impossible. No one can do this.* However, if everyone thought like that, there would be no inventions in science, no innovations in technology, and no breakthroughs in human accomplishment in the different areas of life.

Remember that scientists were baffled when they took a look at the humble bumblebee. Theoretically, they said, it was impossible for the bumblebee to fly. Fortunately for the bumblebee, no one had told it so. So fly it does.

On the other hand, some people suffer from paralysing fear and are unable to act on anything. The result is broken dreams and aspirations in tatters.

If you limit yourself with self-doubt, and self-limiting assumptions, you will never be able to break past what you deem impossible. If you reach too far out into the sky without working towards your desired goal, you will find yourself clinging on to the impossibility.

Try the following exercise.

Exercise: Achieving the impossible

Take a piece of paper and divide it into three columns. Add the following headings:

- Things I know I can do.

- Things I might be able to do.

- Things I cannot do.

Consider your goals, those things you want to achieve in life, and aim to list at least five things (more is good) under each heading.

Now strive every day to do something to bring you closer to accomplishing the goals that are listed under 'Things I know I can do'. When you achieve one, cross it off the list. As you gradually are able to check off all of your goals under that heading, try taking steps to accomplish the goals you listed under the 'Things I might be able to do'.

As those goals are accomplished, look again at the ones you listed under 'Things I cannot do'. Can you move any of them up to one of the other two columns, now that you have learned and accomplished so much?

As you work through this process, you will discover that the goals you thought were impossible become easier to accomplish, and the impossible begins to seem possible after all.

You see, the technique here is not to limit your imagination by negative thinking. It is to aim high, and start working towards that goal little by little to progress and improve your studies. Those who fear most without working hard end up disappointed and disillusioned with life.

Had you told someone two hundred years ago that it was possible for man to walk on the moon, they would have laughed at you. If you had told them that you could send information from here to the other side of the world in a few seconds, they would have said you were out of your mind. And yet, through sheer desire and perseverance, these impossible dreams are now realities.

Thomas Edison once said that genius is one per cent inspiration and 99 per cent perspiration.

Nothing could be more true. For someone to accomplish his or her dreams there has to be hard work and discipline.

Ask any successful student, and he or she will tell you that there can be no gain unless you are regularly moving out of your comfort zone. Remember the sayings 'Nothing happens until something happens' and 'No pain, no gain'? These are eternal truths.

So fear not, friend! Don't get caught up with your perceived limitations and negative beliefs. Think big and work hard to attain those things that your academic heart desires. As you move up the ladder of progress, you will find out that the impossible has just become a little bit more possible.

Last words

Sometimes you may start to suspect that some people are born leaders or are naturally positive thinkers. While some people may simply be more inclined to be positive or negative in their outlook, being positive and staying positive is also a choice that you make. Building self-concept and drawing up plans for self-improvement is an active choice, not predestination or innate talent.

In life, it can be hard to stay focused and positive, especially when situations and people around you keep pulling you down. To combat this, you need to be prepared and have the right tools in your toolbox to help you to cope. It is these tools that we are going to examine in Chapter 3: 'Offering support to individual students'. They are skills and habits that can assist you in all areas of life.

Building self-concept will eventually and inevitably lead to self-improvement as you start to become responsible for who you are, what you have, and what you do. It's like a flame that should gradually spread like a brush fire from inside to outside. When you develop self-concept, you take control of your mission, values and discipline. Self-belief can bring about self-improvement, accurate self-assessment and self-determination.

So how do you start assembling the building blocks of self-concept? Be positive. Be contented and happy. Be appreciative. Never miss an opportunity to give a compliment. A positive outlook will help you to build self-esteem, your starter guide to self-improvement.

Exercise

Almost everyone has room for improvement in some area of their life, whether due to unrealistic expectations, faulty thinking due to previous poor experiences, or an incorrect belief that something is subject to an external LOC and therefore outside of their control.

Think of all the bad habits that are holding you back from fulfilling your true potential and write them out. Re-read the section entitled 'Six positive steps towards breaking a bad habit'. Make a decision and list your plans to change those habits for the better.

Decision + Positive Mindset + Hard Work = Success.

Chapter 3: Offering support to individual students

Taking responsibility for your studies

As a student, it is your responsibility to ensure that you complete your work on time, prepare for tests and exams, and set time aside for dedicated study and learning. It may be that in the past you have had considerable unasked-for external support for such activities — even if only in the form of a nagging parent or teacher — but you have now reached a stage where the responsibility is yours alone.

Chances are that sounds pretty daunting, and that is understandable. Yet by simply taking a strategic step-by-step approach, it can be both relatively straightforward and a pleasure to get organised and take full charge of your situation.

Three cornerstones of success

There are three things to take into account when you are shouldering the responsibility for your academic success (although this approach will serve you well in other areas of your life too).

First, understand why you are doing what you are doing. Identify your core motivation so that when things get tough you can set your sights on your ultimate destination.

Next, set some goals that support you in attaining what you want. You will set study goals later; these may be thought of more as life goals or stepping stones to help you get from where you are now to where you ultimately want to be.

Lastly, devise and establish a support system. This may or may not involve anyone other than yourself.

It's probably worth mentioning that while I have listed these in a particular order and will go on to discuss them in that same order, you might be in a position to establish your support system before you have fully defined your ultimate motivation or supporting goals. That's fine; do this in whatever order suits you best. But think of these three things as the legs of a stool: without all three in place, you're in danger of toppling over.

Cornerstone 1: Understand why you are doing what you are doing

Three labourers were asked what they were doing. 'Breaking rocks,' said the first. 'Earning a living,' said the second. 'Building a cathedral,' said the third. Which of these had a long-term vision and understood why he was doing what he was doing?

Successful people have often said that they had a clear vision of what they wanted to achieve, and that they always kept it in their mind's eye. It gave them the drive and direction they needed to get what they wanted out of life. As a self-motivated person, you will need this kind of dedication and tenacity too.

There are so many distractions, opportunities and temptations that it can be hard to maintain focus and stick to a study schedule, especially when your friends are all taking time out to socialise and have fun. Sticking to a regular schedule is tough and the temptation to say, 'One missed study session won't ruin things; I can easily catch up,' will at times be intense. And it's true: one missed study session every now and then won't ruin things, and sometimes it's nice to do something spontaneous.

However, the danger is that one missed session can become two, then three, or arguably worse: become a regular thing. If you suddenly start attending a pub quiz every Thursday evening, whereas your study schedule has Thursday as a regular study night, that could have serious repercussions. It may be that you can swap it with another evening that was previously 'free', but it may be that you don't feel you can give up any of your other social commitments.

It's at times like this in particular, when choices and sometimes sacrifices have to be made, that it can really help to know that you are building a ca-thedral rather than breaking rocks.

What are you aiming for?

Most of us have dreams and ambitions. Frequently these are material: we think in terms of a luxury apartment or a big house, lots of money, a great car, regular holidays. Other dreams have to do with status, fame and gaining the admiration of our peers. Maybe our dream is to inspire and help others through teaching or writing. Whatever form they take, to turn those dreams and ambitions into reality takes courage, commitment and determination.

Take a moment now to think about what your overarching ambition is. Is it to become a surgeon or nurse? A best-selling author? To be on the board of a FTSE 100 company? The managing director of your own business? A professor of your particular discipline? A scientist making ground-breaking discoveries?

Set your sights high: this is your long-term aim, your over-arching goal, the thing that you are working towards now, but that is likely to take years to achieve. And here's why it's important to look long-term: you probably won't deny yourself many nights out or lazy Sunday afternoons if the cost is simply that you hand an essay in a little late or get a slightly lower grade in a test, but what if your actions could jeopardise your life's ambition?

Is it still worth it, or will you knuckle down and do some studying, as per your schedule?

Cornerstone 2: Set some goals that support you in attaining what you want

You're going to move on to set some interim goals now, and you're going to do that with your overarching goal — your ultimate motivator when things get tough — in mind. These interim goals should support your achievement of that. What you are doing is adding some detail to the picture.

Let's say your overall goal is to become a professor of physics. There are certain things that you will need to do first. First, you need to have achieved the necessary qualifications at GCSE and A level, followed by becoming an undergraduate student at university. You will need to achieve:

- A bachelor's degree.
- A master's degree.
- A doctorate.

Looking at that, you have somewhere between seven and nine years of studying ahead of you, after which you can start aiming for a professorship (although you are unlikely to attain such a position immediately).

If you wish to join the board of a major company, then your path may be as follows:

- A bachelor's degree in a business discipline.
- Several years of work experience.
- An MBA.
- More work experience.

As you can see, this also will take many years to achieve.

Consequently, while you will keep your focus on the overarching objective, you need to be able to break down your main goal into smaller steps in order to make it achievable.

Step one will be to pass the first year of your degree course. That may be broken down further into study goals and targets for the required grades to be achieved. That pattern will be repeated for at least the next year, and possibly longer, depending upon the duration of your degree course.

The final year will include goals for achieving the highest degree you are able to, in order to facilitate your next move.

Cornerstone 3: Devise and establish a support system

Taking responsibility for your learning can be very difficult to do. You will often be learning alone and in those circumstances motivation can be low. Research shows that many people learn better when learning in the company of others or when supported in some way. While it is likely that your university will have a student services body that is able to help, you have to take the first step and approach them to see what they can do for you. Be open-minded to the idea of study groups, mentors and student support services: they may be able to offer a great deal of very valuable help and support to you. Taking advantage of these things is not a sign of weakness, but of strength; accepting that there are times when help is needed and actively seeking out that help is a positive step.

Some psychologists describe the concept of our 'self' as an 'internal community'. They assert that 'who we are' comprises a group of different sub-personalities, each with different skills and abilities to bring to a situation, and that these sub-personalities are directed by an overall controller.

In addition to this internal community, you have an external community of support that you can call upon to help you in your day-to-day tasks. This community consists not only of people — tutors, family, friends, etc. — but also of attitudes and feelings: about films, music, books, politics, current affairs and so on.

When you are learning, it can help to identify what parts of this community or support system will help you to achieve your goals. Obviously, you will need time to learn and understand, but it may be that you learn best in familiar surroundings, with music playing in the background, or in situations where you have to learn because failure to learn is a failure to succeed.

Where tangible support is unavailable, you also need confidence, a sense of self-belief. Build up your own self-belief by setting yourself targets and by taking on new experiences a few at a time. Don't set yourself up for failure by attempting too much in one go. Set yourself achievable targets for learning. As you meet each target, your confidence in your ability to learn will grow and your self-concept will be strengthened.

Reward and celebrate your success

To acknowledge your successes and reward yourself for meeting targets is a robust and valuable element of a support strategy. You can do this in many ways — by buying yourself a small present, having a trip out, making a visit to friends, or simply by congratulating yourself. Reward strategies can also involve simply learning something new so that learning in itself becomes a reward.

Visualise your success

When we take in information, we tend to absorb more via what we see than by any of the other senses; this makes visualisation a very powerful tool.

Begin by closing your eyes and calling to mind a happy event. It could be winning a race at a school sports day, getting your exam results and finding you have done better you expected to, a special birthday celebration, an enjoyable holiday, so long as it is something that means a great deal to you.

Now remember how you felt, how you looked, what you could see, what you could hear, who you were with... Are you smiling yet? Visualisation — viewing a memory on our internal cinema screen — makes things real for us.

You can use this technique to look forward instead of back and visualise yourself as you would like to be. See yourself with all your ambitions realised — picture all the details. Think about not only the fruits of your academic success: your job, status and standing in the community, and all the trappings which that success will bring. Where do you live? Who do you live with? What do you drive? How do you dress? Once you have done this successfully, you have a movie you can watch in your imagination, in the same way as you view your memories, whenever you need a boost or a reminder of why you are doing what you are doing.

Exercise

What is your overarching goal?

We can take real and positive steps towards achieving our ambitions by taking a little time to think about and understand them fully, then breaking things down into more manageable steps. We can start by asking ourselves the following questions:

- What would give my life true meaning and value?

- What would enable me to feel satisfied with what I have achieved at the end of each day?

- What would allow me to approach each new day with a very real sense of purpose?

Take some time to think carefully about this; this is what you will be working hard over the next several years to achieve, so make sure you understand fully why you are doing it and what is in it for you.

Over time your list is likely to evolve and become more refined, and you will find that a clearer picture begins to emerge. Keep your list safe and look at it regularly; this will help you to maintain your focus and commitment. *What's most important to you? Is what you are doing the right way to go about achieving your overarching ambition?*

Set realistic goals + Take steps to move towards them daily.

Chapter 4: Organising and managing your studying

Making the most of your available study time and ensuring that you spend it effectively is a skill that can be learned. It is something that, with a little effort, will become a habit. It's a habit worth developing as your effectiveness here can have a dramatic impact on other areas of your life, in terms of both the free time you have to spend doing other things that you enjoy and your ultimate results, which can in turn have an impact on your status and earning potential for the rest of your life.

Understand where your time goes

Perhaps the best place to start is to try to understand where it is that your time actually goes. We all have had days that start full of promise and end in disappointment, as the tasks we set ourselves to do remain untouched. We rarely do anything else terribly useful either, and so it's a double waste of time.

One thing you might find useful to create is to log your time. Whether you do this for a whole week (for example) or just for your dedicated study periods is up to you. Do whatever will be most useful for you.

Make up a table, putting the days you will be monitoring along the top and blocks of time — in 15 or 30 minute increments — down the side.

Record what you do during each time period. Make a note not only of what you achieve during the course of the exercise, but also such things as the time you spend checking emails, Facebook and Twitter, making coffee, staring into space and playing games. Be honest if you do complete a time log: after all, the purpose is to learn something about where your time goes; being less than frank would make the whole exercise pointless.

Major threats to your success

You may start your day (or your dedicated study period) armed with a detailed 'to do' list and full of enthusiasm and determination, but end it having achieved nothing. Some of the reasons for this are:

- Distraction.
- Interruptions.
- Absent-mindedness.
- Procrastination.
- What's measured is time, not results.
- There's no end in sight.

Do any of those sound familiar to you? If so, let's take a closer look and consider what we can do to stay on track.

Distraction

Even with the best of intentions, one of our biggest time-thieves is distraction. It can take real discipline to keep distractions in check, but there are also a number of tools and techniques you can use to help maintain your focus.

A very useful little technique you can use to try to stay on track is to regularly ask yourself: 'What should I be doing right now?' If you're lucky, the answer will be 'Exactly what I am doing.' If the answer is anything different: stop doing it and get back on track.

It's a simple trick, but it can be surprisingly effective.

Another method is to schedule in times when you can check your emails or have a quick browse around the websites that interest you. If, for example, you regularly check the news, Facebook or the sports results on the Internet, then by having set times, or using a couple of minutes to look at something as a reward for completing a task, you can avoid wasting a couple of hours effectively doing nothing.

Interruptions

Interruptions warrant a mention here too. Not everyone will treat your dedicated study period with the respect it deserves. Friends, relatives and house-mates may all have their own ideas about when you should be available and how you should spend your time. There is nothing wrong with having a set time each day or each week when you 'go dark', becoming unavailable and digitally out of reach, in order to focus specifically on your studying.

Absent-mindedness

Most of us are absent-minded from time to time, but even occasional bouts of absent-mindedness can impact heavily on our time. Useful ways to guard against it include:

- *Make lists.* Making lists is a key part of the planning process. Some people advocate having just one rolling 'to do' list, where new tasks are added to the bottom and completed ones ticked off from the top. Others start the day (or the week) with a list that they rewrite at regular intervals, to remove completed items and make it easier to follow. An alternative method is to use a Gantt chart (more on this later) to show at a glance what needs to be done over a period of time, then split that down into weekly and daily 'to do' lists. Try out various methods and use whatever works for you.

- *Organise the material logically.* Place concepts and terminology logically on the page. Organise the information that you collect into patterns, so that you may understand it better. File your pages in a logical order or one that is clear to you. That way when you need something, it should be obvious where you will find it.

- *Most important of all — concentrate fully on what you are doing.* This might seem self-evident, but sometimes the simple act of concentration is half the battle when it comes to working effectively

Procrastination

Procrastination is a displacement activity in which, instead of doing what we know we should be doing, we do something else, generally easier or more pleasurable, instead. Schraw, Wadkins, and Olafson (2007) contend that three criteria should be in play in order for a behaviour to be classified as 'procrastination': it must be counterproductive, needless, and delaying.

There is a whole raft of reasons why we may procrastinate, including:

- Fear of failure.

- Fear of success.

- Uncertainty as to how to proceed.

- Lack of understanding of the task.

- We believe we do our best work under pressure, so we don't buckle down until the deadline is in sight.

Gallagher, Golin, and Kelleher (1992) conducted a study that showed that over half of students surveyed (52 per cent) indicated having a moderate to high need for help with regard to dealing with procrastination. Fortunately there are positive steps we can take to help us to combat procrastination. Let's take a closer look.

- **Step 1: Be aware** — Awareness is crucial if we are to succeed. We need to be aware of ourselves, our environment, and everything that might impact upon either or both. Self-awareness is vital to success. Knowing your strengths and playing to them is important; knowing your weaknesses and working to combat or improve on them is essential.

- **Step 2: Know your 'prime time'** — We each have a time period during the day when we are most alert, most productive and get the most done. For some people that's first thing in the morning; others need to ease themselves into the day and have highly productive afternoons. There's no right or wrong, but there can be a real advantage in being aware of when you are at your best, allowing you to focus on more complex tasks during those hours.

- **Step 3: Be realistic** — Don't write yourself a 'to do' list that you simply cannot complete. By all means make it challenging, but if it is impossible, and you know it is impossible, it may very well cause you to not even try to get anything done. There is only so much you can do, even when working at peak efficiency. Acknowledge this, and set your goals and targets accordingly.

- **Step 4: Know the cost of time-wasting** — If you spend time during a scheduled study period doing something other than studying, then make sure it is worth your while. Whatever you don't do now, you will have to do at some other time, and you might find that the only time you have available is precious and/or costly. What if it means you have to take time off from a part-time job? What if it means you can't afford the time to go the cinema at the weekend? What if you have to miss a social event you've been looking forward to? Count the cost of giving in to the lure of doing something easier or more pleasurable now or you might regret it later.

- **Step 5: Use the 80/20 rule to your advantage** — Many people are aware of this simple but very valid rule (also known as the Pareto principle): 20 per cent of a sales force achieve 80 per cent of the sales; 20 per cent of customers account for 80 per cent of profits; 20 per cent of your effort produces 80 per cent of your results. This isn't a green light for spending 80 per cent of our time deliberately unproductively, however; rather, it is a warning that if we are not careful, we can lose hours every week trying to make things perfect, and perfectionism is a trap. Know when to stop and move on.

Use this knowledge to your advantage and you will get more done.

The 80/20 rule principle applied

Successful students often use the power of the Pareto Principle. They may spend less time studying than more average students and yet achieve better grades, that is, 80 per cent of their results come from 20 per cent of their efforts. Thus, instead of working for five hours a day, the best students may only work for two. The difference is that the best students are properly focusing their efforts. They are putting in two hours of concentrated study, eliminating all distractions and focusing on the proper 20 per cent of their workload. They invest more time on the most important things that they see as the priority, which will give them 80 per cent of the results that they want. These students are willing to put their best effort into whatever they do on a daily basis. Their first goal is to know more about their chosen field. In any field, the more knowledge you acquire and the more practice you gain, the more competent and respected you become. As you get better at you studies, your ability increases across all your subjects.

In contrast, more average students appear to study for longer, yet they are not as focused. They tend to make little effort to improve their skills and academic performance; they seldom bother to go through their lecture notes or do the recommended readings. Their lack of interest and nonchalant attitude impedes their productive ability in their studies (Cottrell, 2003). As a result, their academic skills fail to improve.

Step 6: Understand Parkinson's Law — According to Cyril Northcote Parkinson, 'Work expands so as to fill the time available for its completion.' So he said and he was undeniably correct. A task takes as long as it takes because it has always taken that long, or because that's how long we have to spend on it: if we have all day to complete a task, then that task will inevitably take us all day. (In reality, it may take us an hour and a half at the end of the day, feeling the pressure and working as fast as we can because we have put it off and given in to distractions before the deadline started to bite).

Multitasking

With the hustle and bustle of modern-day life, it can be very difficult to achieve your dreams. As day-to-day tasks take their toll and life takes over, even setting and working towards your goals can be a challenge. Increasingly students are having to multi-task to fit more activities and tasks into their day with ever increasing efficiency.

What is multitasking?

Multitasking refers to a person's ability to handle more than one task at the same time. When a person multitasks, they undertake numerous tasks simultaneously such as watching television, listening to the audio player and preparing dinner. Many high-school students routinely media multitask while studying. Students can often be observed using Facebook and texting while studying, thereby dividing their attention between their academic works and communication with their friends. On average, during one-third of the time that they are reading and during half of the time that they spend completing homework on computer, they are also using at least two other forms of electronics media (Hembrooke & Gay, 2003).

The detrimental impact of multitasking on academic performance

Multitasking in the context of studying has been found to have a negative impact on academic performance and learning. Teachers have contended that the widespread use of social media by students is damaging to students' academic performance. Similarly, Wood et al. (2012) found that multitasking had a negative effect on learning. They found that students who used Facebook while attending a lecture scored significant lower on tests of the lecture material than those who were only allowed to take notes in the lecture using paper and pen. This suggests that students who do not use technology during a lecture tend to outperform students who use technology during lecture.

What studies say about multitasking and educational performance

Junco and Cotton (2011) studied students who reported spending relatively large amounts of time on instant messaging and engaging in instant messaging while doing schoolwork. They found that multitasking has a detrimental effect on educational performance. Distractions in the study context tend to weaken brain power, since they place demands on the cognitive system in such a way that overall academic performance suffers.

A recent study by Rosen et al. (2011) found that students who receive instant text-message interruptions during class performed poorly in tests.

Studies in cognitive psychology provide insight into what happens when students multitask. Mental overload occurs when learning task exceed the processing capacity of the reasoning system. In other words, attempting to attend to or process more than one task at a time overloads the capacity of the human information system. Mayer and Moreno (2003) distinguish between three types of cognitive demand, namely: essential processing, incidental processing and representational holding.

1. **Essential processing** is the basic cognitive process required for making sense of presented material, including selecting and organising words and images from the presented materials and integrating those words and images in a meaningful manner.

2. **Incidental processing** refers to the cognitive processes that are not essential for making sense of the presented materials, but because their presence also requires processing, it contributes to total cognitive demand.

3. **Representational holding** refers to processes that hold mental representations of the study material in working memory.

Also researching cognitive overload, Asplund et al. (2011), found that participants respond more slowly on dual task trials than on single task trials, for both visual-manual and auditory-vocal tasks, and they have poorer accuracy.

Way forward

Multitasking requires much attention; the inability of students to pay attention to schoolwork will limit their cognitive input, thereby impeding the quality of their studying, the amount and rate of their learning, and their academic results.

Given the overwhelming evidence of the detrimental effects of multitasking on studying and learning, we should practice focusing on one task until completion, rather than doing many things simultaneously with only partial attention and fractured intention. Desire for academic excellence can only be achieved by a firm decision to remain focused on one activity at a time. In addition to modifying one's attentional control by switching off social media while learning, developing sound study habits can facilitate the learning process.

What's measured is time, not results

If your plan for a study period is to spend two hours on topic A and one hour on topic B, then you might get to the end of the three hour period having learned nothing. The reason for this is that you are measuring time, not results.

You are likely to have far more success if your plan reads as follows:

- Topic A: read chapters 1 to 4. Make notes in the form of a notation map to help remember the information. Copy out relevant quotes with references for future use.

- Topic B: Revise notation maps from last Tuesday's lecture.

Do you see the difference? This way, not only will you devote time to your study, but you will be measuring the outcome, the positive result you are looking for, and that will help you to achieve your goals.

There's no end in sight

If what you need to learn and to understand seems to stretch out before you to infinity, then it can seem futile — or even impossible — to make a start. The trick here is to break the task down into manageable bite-sized pieces. Let's say you have just embarked on a business management course.

It is too open-ended to have as a goal 'learn about business management'. That is such a huge target that it is, in itself, meaningless.

If, however, rather than doing that you look at the syllabus and pull out some of the individual topics (leadership, project planning, financial management, for example) then that starts to make things more manageable. Then you can begin to break down what you need to know about each topic. So financial management may be split down into understanding the financial statements, understanding and using ratios, setting targets, financial forecasting, and so on.

From there you can drill down further, splitting 'understanding the financial statements' into 'balance sheet', 'profit and loss statement', 'cash flow' and so on. In that way you take a huge, amorphous goal and make it tangible and relevant. Now you can spend an hour studying balance sheets and know that you have taken a positive step towards your goal of achieving a degree in a business discipline.

Look after yourself — And finally, a word to the wise: take care of yourself. The reason is simple: if you are tired, run down or unwell, you cannot do your best work, and the work you do will take you longer to complete. Things you try to learn will not 'stick'. Try to avoid 'burn-out' by applying a little common sense: eat well, get some exercise, get enough sleep, and balance time spent studying with time doing other things, time spent with family and friends with time spent alone, time spent fulfilling your obligations to others with time spent doing what matters to you. There will be times when we have to act out of equilibrium — that's life — but whenever possible, do try to maintain some balance in your life.

How to get results

You'll be familiar by now with the 'steps' approach that has been taken throughout this study guide to make information more manageable and more easily assimilated. It should come as no surprise that, when we are focusing specifically on how to get results, we again advocate breaking things down into manageable parts and taking a step-by-step approach to success.

In Chapter 5 'How to excel by using the right techniques', we will consider in detail how to use techniques that enhance our chances of success. What we are going to do here is to examine what needs to be done in order to boost your chances of getting the results you desire.

Get organised

There's no getting away from the fact that good organisation is the key to keeping on top of everything you have to do. It may be that your organisational skills are pretty good already, or it may be that you are starting to develop them from a fairly rudimentary standpoint. Either way, these rules and guidelines will keep you on the right track.

The steps we are going to follow are:

- **Step 1:** Organise your workspace.

- **Step 2:** Get a diary.

- **Step 3:** Make a list.

Let's take a look at those in a little more detail.

Step 1: Organise your workspace

Don't kid yourself that a genius can work in chaos; very, very few people can. And if your desk and your study area are a mess, then just the thought of it can put you off using it. If there is no clear surface on which to spread books and notes, or even just to place your laptop, then you're stopped before you start.

Take a little time to keep things clear and to make sure you always have what you need to hand, whether that be pens, paper, technology or anything else. Tidy up when you finish work and leave it ready for the next session. Make this a habit.

Step 2: Get a diary

It doesn't have to be a diary in the usual sense, but you do need something with days and dates on it. It can be electronic or paper, whichever suits you, but you definitely need one.

The first reason you need one is so that you can mark specific events on it. These should be both study-related and social. This is key: if your deadline to complete an essay falls on the same day as your best friend's birthday, then the chances are you need to make sure that the essay is finished beforehand so you can join in with the celebrations. If you are asked to attend a party the evening before an important test or exam, then you can make a decision as to how to handle that. But you will know well in advance, not be caught out a day or two beforehand and thrown into a panic.

The second reason you need a diary is that it will help you to complete step 3.

Step 3: Make a list

When you create your 'to do' list — or lists, depending on how you decide to work — you need to make sure you take into account all the elements of a task in time to meet your deadline accordingly

1. Start early

2. Understand the assignment

3. Have a plan

4. Be creative

5. Develop an outline

Review related requirements

For example, if you see from your diary that you have an essay due in three weeks' time, you need to schedule in time for:

- Research and reading.

- Analysis of the results of the research.

- Structuring the essay in terms of headings and weighting of information.

- Writing up a first draft.

- Revision and proofreading.

Break down tasks into their component parts and you can then schedule each one, making sure none are missed out. It can be quite common to get so involved with research that we cut ourselves short of time for subsequent activities. Taking this approach will ensure that you allocate an amount of time and a deadline to each element of a task.

Note: There is more information about 'to do' lists in the 'Planning techniques' section in Chapter 5.

Exercise

Look again at the three steps outlined above in the section headed 'Get organised'. Make a start by ensuring that your workspace is clear, tidy and well-equipped, then sort out a diary and begin to make a 'to do' list for the next four weeks. Add items to it as and when new things come up, and always work as far ahead as you need to in order to accommodate your responsibilities, whether that be the four weeks I suggest you start with, a full study term, or longer.

Hard work aligns you for excellence
+ Follow your To-Do List.

Chapter 5: How to excel by using the right techniques

In order to excel as a student, good study skills are crucial. As well as knowing what to do, you need to know how to do it, and how to use a range of established planning and management techniques to your advantage.

The techniques we're about to discuss fall into four categories:

- Maximising time.

- Planning techniques.

- Preparing to learn.

- Memory enhancers.

Maximising time

We talked a lot in the previous section about those things that steal our time and how we might be able to fight them, but is there any way we can make more time available?

Time is both linear and finite. Once this moment has gone, it cannot be recovered and used again. You can't save up time for a rainy day. All you can do is make the most of what there is.

Two techniques you can use to maximise the time available are time-framing and waking early.

Time-framing

Time framing can be a useful technique when you are struggling to get started with something, especially if it's a large task that just needs to have a start made to get it underway, or something you find to be a tedious chore. Rather than lose time by dithering or deciding to put that particular task to one side and do something else instead, simply set yourself a fixed period of time, say half an hour, to make a dent in it. Don't worry about how far you get, simply commit to spending that amount of time working on that one thing.

A possible side effect is that you may end up getting into the job after all and working much longer than originally planned. And if you don't, that's fine, because not only have you made a start, you also gave yourself permission to stop after only half an hour.

Waking up early

Is there any chance you could get up an hour earlier, maybe even two, in the morning?

Most of us keep the hours we do out of habit, but habits can be changed. While it is essential that you get enough sleep, is it possible that you are being indulgent with your current sleeping pattern?

If you think that this is something that might work for you, then there are two techniques you can use to change your routine; gradual reduction of sleeping hours, or quick change.

Gradual reduction has the advantage that you can build up to your desired rising time, moving the clock back by, say, fifteen minutes each week until you hit your target.

With quick change, as the name suggests, you go straight to the new time. It'll probably take a couple of weeks for it to become a habit and you may well feel like giving up, but if the motivation is strong enough, you'll do it.

If you feel that while you might be able to get up earlier, you couldn't face studying at that time of the morning, think about what you might do instead. Say you usually go for a run later in the day, could you try going for your run first thing? That will help you to wake up and you'll have your previous running time free for study.

Another option, if you're more night owl than lark, is to get up at the same time, but go to bed a little later instead. If you do this, make sure you use the time you gain for studying and not something else!

Planning techniques

The chances are that you are going to be juggling a number of projects and assignments at the same time. You therefore need ways of keeping track of what has been done, what is still to do, and how you are progressing.

At the end of Chapter 4 'Organising and managing your studying', I discussed the need to get organised and identified three distinct steps that were necessary. Those steps were:

- **Step 1:** Organise your workspace.

- **Step 2:** Get a diary.

- **Step 3:** Make a list.

The following planning techniques are going to assume that you have taken care of Step 1 and will focus on how to make the most of Steps 2 and 3.

There are a number of planning techniques you can use and you can make it as complicated or as simple as you wish. We're going to focus on three distinct areas here:

- Setting SMART objectives.

- Using Gantt charts.

- Using dynamic 'to do' lists.

Setting SMART objectives

Would you consider setting out on a long journey without knowing exactly where you were going, how you would get there and how long it would take? What you do in life is no different: if you don't know where you're headed on life's journey, you should not be surprised if you end up somewhere totally different to the place you had hoped to be.

Our *destinations* when we plan our study periods and in our private lives can be called *goals* or *objectives.* The *directions* are the *plans* we make to get us there, and en route we use *milestones and monitoring techniques* to check that we are still on course.

Goals may be set for the short, medium and long term. Your study goals will normally be communicated to you by your tutor and they will also be influenced by your own ambition. Such goals might include: complete an essay on the works of William Shakespeare; prepare for a test on project planning techniques; revise for an end-of-year exam. Your personal goals will depend on what you want to achieve in your life. Some of them will be career-orientated: pass this year of my course; establish a robust study schedule; achieve a first class degree. Others might be: learn to ski; pay off my credit card bill; lose weight. All of them become more tangible when you apply a deadline and break the goal down into manageable steps.

Goals and objectives should be SMART, which may be defined as:

- **S**pecific: very clearly defined.

- **M**easurable: there must be a way that we are able to prove that we have met them.

- **A**chievable: we should be able to visualise success, it may well be challenging but it should be within our grasp.

- **R**ealistic: we should only ever set objectives that it is possible for us to meet.

- **T**imed: there should always be a deadline by which an objective should have been met.

In addition to thinking SMART, the following tips are useful for setting effective goals:

- *Stretch yourself.* There is little sense of achievement to be enjoyed by doing what you already know you can do. You probably derive a sense of satisfaction from using and demonstrating well-honed skills and abilities, but this isn't the place for that behaviour.

- *Be realistic.* 'Challenging' is wholly different to 'impossible'. When you set goals, you should set goals you can feasibly achieve; that way you develop skills and knowledge and grow as a person. If your goals are too lofty and you know they are too lofty, then you have deliberately set yourself up to fail. That's destructive and self-defeating. Don't do it.

- *Be specific.* If a study goal is 'to pass the test', what grade or score do you want to achieve? If a personal goal is 'to lose weight', how much do you want to lose? Be very clear as to how you will measure success, otherwise your goals lack clarity and meaning.

- *Set a deadline by which you will attain your goal.* Again, be realistic; some things take more time than others. Your study goal might now read: 'To pass every end-of-term test with a top-five per cent score'. Your personal goal might be: 'To lose ten pounds by my next birthday'. Now you have a specific goal you can aim for rather than a vague desire to achieve something, and a time at which you will either celebrate your success or review the situation and work out why you failed to achieve your goal. Was it unrealistic? Did you fail to try hard enough? Be honest when you evaluate the outcome and aim to learn from the whole experience.

- *Tell someone.* Whether it's your tutor or a friend, make a firm commitment to action. If you don't, then you can quietly drop it if you don't buckle down and do the work, but you will carry a sense of failure which may damage your self-concept.

- *Know why you are doing it.* Identify the benefits of success. There will very likely be days when it all feels like very hard work and knowing *why* you are doing something — like playing your visualisation film on your internal cinema screen or putting a picture of yourself before you gained the weight you are now trying to lose on the fridge door — can help to keep you focused on the end result, especially if hitting this goal will help you move closer to achieving another. Try always to be aware of the impact of your actions on the big picture. These are early steps of what will be a long journey

Using Gantt charts

Your diary will help you to create a Gantt chart, which will in turn highlight for you times when you will be especially busy, or perhaps less so and will be able to devote time to catching up, getting ahead or exploring subjects that interest you in more depth.

Devised by and named after Henry Gantt in around 1910, the Gantt chart is a simple but powerful tool designed for project planners and work schedulers. A Gantt is a horizontal bar chart that provides an at-a-glance overview of a project, highlighting dependencies and milestones and showing how long each task requires and, more importantly, how much time it has available to it for completion.

Consider this example:

TASKS	WEEKS								
	1	2	3	4	5	6	7	8	9
Essay on the works of Shakespeare	▓	▓	▓						
Essay on the works of Kant			▓	▓	▓	▓	▓		
Prepare for English test	▓	▓							
Prepare for philosophy test			▓	▓	▓				
Revise for end-of-year exam						▓	▓	▓	▓

Obviously this is a very simple example, but you can see at a glance where commitments overlap and also that week 3 promises to be both busy and varied. If it helps, you can use a colour coding system so that for essays, for example, you have one colour for research, another for analysis of material and a third for writing.

Gantts can be prepared over any time period. You can have one that shows a year, a term, a month or even just a week. Use it in whatever way is useful to you. It is a tool and you should adapt it to your needs.

There is one thing that a Gantt doesn't do, and that is to indicate the magnitude of a task. You can see how long something will take to complete, but not what percentage of the time that is available to you it will require. Your revision, for example, might have three hours a week devoted to it for the first three weeks, then six for the final two, but your Gantt won't show you that.

The way that you can take it all into account is by using your Gantt to prepare detailed 'to do' lists.

Using 'to do' lists

I would recommend preparing two sets of lists from your Gantt. The first would be taken straight from the chart and would show in a little more detail than the Gantt allows regarding what you need to do on a weekly basis (e.g. you can indicate hours of work or number of pages to be read or words to be written). The second would show those tasks allocated to specific times on a daily (or per study period) basis. Any social events that will impact upon study time should also be noted here.

It's a simple system but surprisingly effective. Again, these are tools for you to use. Try this system and if it doesn't quite work for you, change things around until you have a system that does.

Preparing to learn

You'll get far more out of your study periods if you can get into the right frame of mind before you start. Here are some simple things you can do to help create a 'learning' frame of mind.

1. Remember why you're learning

Earlier you prepared a visualisation film that you could play on your internal cinema screen. Take a minute or two before you settle down to study to remember what you are working towards. Having your ultimate motivation in mind will help you to approach the task ahead in a positive manner.

2. Use affirmations

Research has shown that people will respond according to how they are treated. If, for example, employees are treated as if they cannot be trusted, they will become less trustworthy. A child consistently told he or she is 'a little monster' will behave accordingly. Affirmations are used by many to reinforce what or how they want to be.

Think of your learning affirmation as positive programming, rather than the negative programming examples given above. Affirmations should state the desired outcome as if it were a fact now, so the phrasing should not be 'I will be ...' or 'I would like ...' but 'I am ...' and 'I can ...' Keep it short and to-the- point and repeat it regularly — for example three times when you wake, three times before you go to sleep and three times before you settle down to study (the more frequently you repeat it, the better; this isn't something you can overdo). While it's a good idea for you to come up with your own learning affirmation, you might consider something along the lines of: 'I am a competent learner'; or, 'I focus on my studies and learn effectively'.

Not everyone is comfortable with using affirmations, but if this is something with which you are happy then you can start straight away.

3. Remind yourself how good you are

To be in college or university, you already have lots of accomplishments to your name. You have excelled in your studies, for a start. It is likely that you have other successes to look back on as well, perhaps sporting achievements or musical prowess. Make a list of your achievements and keep it handy. If you begin to feel overwhelmed or that you aren't up to the task ahead of you, look at the list and you'll get an instant boost.

And always remember: the best way to get lots of things done is to focus on and complete one task at a time.

Memory enhancers

In addition to getting into the right frame of mind, there are a host of other tricks and techniques you can use to help you to remember what you learn. Here are some that you might find useful.

Memory boosters

Our brains have an incredible capacity for memory and we can develop little tricks and techniques to boost this to our advantage.

Mnemonics

A mnemonic is any learning technique that aids information retention. Often it is a pattern of letters or words, which is used to aid the memory. You may be familiar with 'Every Good Boy Deserves Favour', which indicates the order of the notes from top to bottom on the treble clef stave or 'Richard Of York Gave Battle In Vain' for the order of the colours in the spectrum (Red, Orange, Yellow, Green, Blue, Indigo, Violet).

Many of the acronyms that are used in modern business also serve as a form of mnemonic, for example SMART objectives (Specific, Measurable, Achievable, Realistic, Timed) or SWOT analysis (Strengths, Weaknesses, Opportunities, Threats).

You can make up your own mnemonics, or you may well come across tried and tested ones that appeal to you and that you can use to your advantage.

Memory joggers

People use all sorts of little memory joggers to keep them on the right track. Some we learn as children in school, such as: 'Thirty days hath September, April, June and November, All the rest have 31, Except February alone which has 28 days clear and 29 in each leap year'. Other 'joggers' can be very simple indeed: for example, if you get 'stationery' and 'stationary' mixed up, just remember that you get your pap*er* from the station*er*.

Exercise

Consider the two techniques described in the 'Maximising time' section above: time-framing and waking early. How can you use time-framing to your advantage? Will you benefit from effectively lengthening your day by either getting up earlier or going to bed later?

If you feel you can extend your day, make a plan as to how you will tackle the change (whether incrementally or in one fell swoop) and commit to its implementation. Make sure you use your extra time wisely!

Identify what works for you
+ Practice taking responsibility.

Chapter 6: Developing the right study method for you

As a student, how exactly will you accomplish what you want for your studies? How will you attain a first-class grade? Equally important, how will you consistently maintain your academic performance?

You have probably heard the ancient adage 'Practice makes perfect'. In the late 1960s Vince Lombardi, the legendary coach of the Green Bay Packers, said, "Practice doesn't make perfect. Only Perfect Practice Makes Perfect". The same applies in education: only the right study method will lead to good results.

No two people learn in exactly the same way. We all have preferences and blind spots and we learn to adapt to whatever is suitable to us.

That's not to say, however, that we shouldn't play to our strengths whenever possible. In order to do that we need to understand how people learn. This will enable you to understand the process you will go through as you study and take on board information. Once we've looked at the different ways people learn, we'll look a little more closely to try to identify your own learning preferences. Once you know what they are you can, wherever possible, tailor your studying and learning activities and methods to suit so that you get the most from your efforts.

Types of learning

There are four main types of learning:

- **Intuitive**: A style of 'learning by osmosis', where we learn without being conscious of doing so (we pick it up as we go along).

- **Incidental**: A more deliberate style of learning, where we are prompted by events to consider what has happened, why, and what it means for us (we learn from our experiences).

- **Retrospective**: This involves looking back on events and learning from them, perhaps reflecting on what was covered in a lecture (we consider what learning means to us).

- **Prospective**: This is planned and active learning, where we decide what we want to learn, why, and how, and then set about doing it (we plan our learning and consolidate it by reviewing it afterwards).

The majority of the learning you will be doing at secondary (high school) and tertiary level (college or university) is prospective, although you will undoubtedly pick up information and knowledge in other ways too. In the case of prospective or planned learning, we can take a systematic and strategic approach. Planning our learning allows us to use what we learn from the learning cycle.

The learning cycle

The learning cycle has four stages: 'plan, do, check, act,' with each continually leading onto the next.

- **Plan**: We plan a learning experience, perhaps by going to a lecture, setting aside some time for studying, or attending a regular study group.

- **Do**: We undertake the experience.

- **Check**: We review and analyse what we learned, either using our own notes or perhaps by discussing it with others. This stage is vital: if we undertake a learning experience without afterwards reinforcing what we learned by referring back to linear notes and/or notation maps and recapping the main points, we will lose that information.

- **Act**: We work out how we can incorporate that learning into our way of doing things, and assess what it is that we need to learn next. This may involve developing complementary skills or digging deeper into the current subject.

The learning cycle is arguably more like a continuous learning spiral, with one cycle leading into the following one as we gain competence in one subject area and then move on to the next.

So we understand that the majority of our learning will be prospective, or planned, and we know that we will get into a continuous learning spiral, where learning and mastering one aspect of a subject will lead us into learning and then mastering the next. But what are our own personal preferences when it comes to learning?

Training and learning specialists Peter Honey and Alan Mumford (2006) explained methods of distinct learning styles:

- **Activists**: learn best from short, intensive, 'hands-on' experiences — 'Let me try that for myself.'

- **Reflectors**: learn best from situations where they can observe and listen — 'Let me absorb it.'

- **Theorists**: learn best from theories or models — 'Explain to me how it would work.'

- **Pragmatists**: learn best when they can clearly see the practical application — 'What's in it for me?'

Learning style

The term 'learning style' refers to the method by which a learner prefers to learn; for example, by active listening, drawing, and/or note-taking. In education, learning styles are less concerned with *what* learners learn than with *how* they prefer to learn. Learning style comprises cognitive, affective and physiological factors that are stable indicators of how an individual learner perceives, interacts with, and responds to his or her learning environment and the learner's learning style is determined by his or her unique abilities. Stewart and Felicetti (1992) describe learning style as those educational conditions under which a student is most likely to learn.

The identification of an individual's preferred style of learning is important for improving students' performance in a variety of contexts. Individual differences in the learner and the learning environment are typically studied within the field of differential psychology, which studies the ways in which individual and group differences in behaviour. Eagle & Chaiken (1993) explain that the psychology of attitudes is based on the psychological processes and cognitive structures of individuals. Bohner & Wanke (2002) suggested that attitudes can also be the product of groups, e.g. stereotypes. The cognitive characteristics of an individual are related to their attitudes in that an individual's attitudes will influence their perception, thinking, behaviour, and actions (LaPiere, 1934; Ajzen, 2001).

Attitudes refer to sentimental assessments of life circumstances while cognitions refer to knowledge and beliefs. Thus, a method of studying needs to focus equally on cognitions (the intellectual content that one is studying) and attitudes (one's motivations towards studying a particular subject).

Assimilating information

While successful learners may all employ strategies that differ to a greater or lesser degree, they all have one thing in common: their approach to learning is active, not passive. They question what they are learning, they test theories, they compare opinions, and they form their own conclusions on the basis of what they read or are told, what they know or believe, and what they can interpret or extrapolate from data.

Irrespective of your preferred learning style (and we will look at learning styles in more detail shortly) there are certain key strategies you can adopt to give yourself the best chance of acquiring and retaining information.

Key strategy 1: Get an overview

Don't go into anything blind. Always try to get an overview of what you will be studying/learning. Look at any existing notes, check things out online or in the library, watch a television programme if one exists. What you're aiming to do here is to see the big picture. Don't worry about the detail at this stage, what you want is to understand the 'shape' of things. If you are reading a book, scope out the contents and layout and get a feel for the style before you dive in and read the whole thing. (There is much more on this in Chapter 7 'The best way to read a book'.)

Key strategy 2: Note down what you already know

As an undergraduate student, it is unlikely that you will be studying a subject about which you have absolutely no prior knowledge. (This is also often true of students at other levels, especially those who are studying at exam level.)

Before you undertake a learning experience, take a little time to note down what you already know. This is especially useful if you feel overwhelmed by what you will be learning. Say you know you are going into a lecture about the romantic poets: spend a little time noting down (for example) who are the most noteworthy, what are their most important works, what defines the style. This has a double benefit: acknowledging your existing knowledge gives your confidence a boost; and the exercise itself gets you into the right 'head space' to learn more.

Also, should you realise as a result of completing the exercise that there are some things of which you are unsure, note them down. Should your lecturer not cover those aspects in the detail you would like, you can ask questions and/or conduct research to flesh out your knowledge.

Key strategy 3: Break down larger tasks into smaller steps

I've mentioned this before and I make no apology for bringing it up again: it is key to your success, not just in learning, but in many other areas of your life too.

If you wish to expand your vocabulary, setting yourself the task of learning one new word a day is both tangible and manageable. If you wish to read *War and Peace*, settling down to ten (or twenty) pages a day gets the job done without completely taking over your available reading time. If you wish to learn to play an instrument, starting with a small number of notes and simple tunes gets you playing, and you can then build up your skill gradually.

This is a vital technique, but you must set yourself achievable daily or weekly objectives. That way, you get to regularly celebrate your successes, which both boosts your self-confidence and acts as a motivator. Don't ever set yourself up to fail by being unrealistic about what you can achieve; small, regular steps will get you to your goal.

Key strategy 4: Constantly question

Small children are known for their questioning, their thirst for knowledge and understanding of the world they live in, prompting them constantly to ask, 'Why?' As a student, this is a habit it pays to adopt.

Don't just blindly accept what you read or are told; critically question the credibility of the source, the implications of the knowledge, the age of the information (has it been superseded by subsequent discoveries?), and how you can use the knowledge to further your own understanding. Always, always, question.

Learning styles

Take a moment to consider what your natural response would be to having something explained to you. Which would you be most likely to say: 'That looks right', 'That sounds right', or 'That feels right'. Whichever response you would make helps to show which of three broad learning styles is likely to suit you best:

1. Visual learners (That looks right, I see what you mean).

2. Auditory learners (That sounds right, I hear what you're saying).

3. Kinaesthetic learners (That feels right, I can handle that).

Let's take a closer look at those styles.

Visual learners: These learners understand taught concepts mainly in terms of visually perceived written materials such as hand-outs, textbooks and other literature visual aids that they can see including words, pictures, diagrams, graphs, maps and charts. They also like to watch demonstrations or videos. It is visual or graphic representations that they remember most easily and assimilate well. These students also tend to have a sharp, clear picture of the experiences that they encounter in the classroom.

Auditory learners: These students tend to learn best by hearing. They prefer to learn through audio tapes, lectures in class, verbal instructions, seminars, debates, discussions, social interaction, and by reading aloud to themselves. They generally remember things that they hear more than things that they see. In class they remember group discussions and participations. This is because they identify sounds related to an experience more than images of the experience.

Kinaesthetic (or tactile) learners: These students learn best through physical experiments in the laboratory and by touching, feeling and experiencing that which they are trying to learn. They like to be involved directly in a hands-on way. Students in this group remember things by writing about or touching the learning object. Through their interaction in the classroom they develop a strong feeling towards the experience.

Strategies for learners

Research conducted by Lynn O'Brien, (1989) director of Specific Diagnostic Studies in Maryland, has revealed that while we all utilise all three learning styles to a greater or lesser degree, most of us do display a preference for one style over the others. By the time we reach adulthood, however, visual preference dominates. She has devised a test you can take to determine your own learning style preference.

We are now going to consider some learning style strategies we can employ in order to ensure we get the most out of our learning. Whatever the form of in which learning you are involved, whether you are a student, parent, teacher or corporate executive, when you understand your learning style and use the right strategy, learning becomes easier and quicker, and it is possible to learn new information more naturally.

Visual strategies

- **Notation maps:** Depicting a topic visually as they do, notation maps are perfect for visual learners. The act of creating them aids learning and retention, and then the maps themselves act as a quick and thorough refresher when revising a subject.

- **Visualisation:** Making a film that you can play on your imaginary cinema screen can be a very effective way of learning. Mental imagery is a powerful technique. Many people with the ability to perform prodigious feats of memory say they use visualisation to help them to remember items on a list, for example, in the right order.

Auditory strategies

Read it out loud: Read what you are learning aloud and make it dramatic; that will help make it memorable. You can use different accents and change the volume up or down to help make information 'stick'.

Join a discussion group: This can be a very useful technique for auditory learners. Not only do you get to explore knowledge and information in your preferred way, but you get insight and input from others as you do so.

Kinaesthetic strategies

Move about while you read or listen: Kinaesthetic learners need to get an element of the physical into their studying and learning and one way in which they can do this is by moving about. Another strategy is to write key words and concepts on sticky notes and arrange them on a board (or even the wall) to help get your thoughts in order.

Make notes: Writing and making notes is a great way to convert passive information-gathering (reading, listening) into physical activity, which will help it to 'stick'.

Combining learning styles

Often students use more than one learning style. A meta-study by Marzano (1998) found that graphic and tactile representations of the subject matter had noticeable effects on learning outcomes for both kinaesthetic/tactile and visual learners. Similarly, Constantinidou and Baker (2002) found that visual presentation through the use of pictures was advantageous not only for those with a visual style of learning but also for most adults who are kinaesthetic/tactile learners. This suggests that, while each learner might have a preferred style, it is possible that the process of producing visual, audio or graphic representations of study materials could be beneficial for all learners regardless of their learning style.

Identifying your own learning style

No two students are alike. No two students learn in an identical way. An style or method that enriches one student's learning does not necessarily enrich that of another. Students should be taught to think for themselves in the classroom. Identify the style or styles that most facilitate your understanding of the concepts being studied.

Working with others

While understanding your preferred learning style will undoubtedly help you to study more effectively, there will also be times when, irrespective of the style you prefer, working with others will benefit you too. In this respect you might consider working with a mentor and/or joining or establishing a study group. Let's take a closer look.

Working with a mentor

A mentor can offer expert advice, specialist knowledge and insightful assistance and help you to keep on track and achieve your learning goals. If you are in a study group, consider asking someone from your group who is further advanced in their studies than you are to be your mentor. Alternatively, one of your lecturers, or perhaps a specialist in your field of study, might be willing to step in. Most universities have a mentor programme and this would very likely be the best place to start.

As you progress in your academic career, be prepared to return the favour for more junior students by acting as a mentor to them in turn.

You should always make a point of seeking external feedback on your performance and progress. If you have a mentor, then some of your feedback will come naturally from that source. Other feedback may come from your test or exam results, your tutor and other lecturers, and your peers. Don't be defensive when you get feedback other than a pat on the back, which points to areas where you could do better. While praise where it is due is always welcome, it is this second, more balanced kind of feedback that we can learn most from.

Joining/establishing a study group

There are times when it can really help to talk things through with fellow students. While that is often likely to happen in an unplanned, unstructured and spontaneous way, being part of a study group with a focus on sharing and consolidating knowledge and learning can be hugely beneficial. Investigate whether a group that would meet your needs already exists. If it does, join it. If it doesn't, seek out some like-minded students and establish a group of your own.

Making notes that help you to learn

One of the core skills that you need to succeed as a student is the ability to make useful, relevant notes. Notes are essential in terms of recording information during lectures, seminars, personal tutorials, group work, research and revision.

If possible, try to record the information first time round in such a way that you don't need to rewrite your notes. However, while you are developing good note-taking skills, you might have to accept that rewriting will be necessary, in which case you can build that requirement into your study plan.

Basic strategies for making notes

We talked a little above about notation maps. Here we are going to focus on linear notes.

- **Be selective** — The most important thing to remember when making your notes is to be selective. In lectures, you can't record every word. When reading, do not copy out large chunks of text as this will not help you to learn the information. Likewise, it is not a good use of your time; you might as well just re-read the original source.

- **Note down questions arising** — Make a note of any questions that occur to you while you are undertaking revision and/or preparation for study. This will help you to identify and address gaps in your knowledge and structure future research and revision periods to cover them.

- **Structure information** — It is important to structure your notes as this will make them easier to use in the future. Use headings, sub-headings and bullet points to break down those parts of your notes which address different aspects of a topic.

- **Highlight key points** — It can be a good idea to use highlighters or coloured pens to make key areas of your notes stand out. However, it is important that you do not overuse the technique, or else you will defeat the purpose of it.

- **Write clearly and legibly** — Whenever you write notes, it is crucial that you lay them out so that they are clear and easy to read. Scrawled, unreadable revision notes are essentially useless. Take a little time to think about how you will format them and lay them out.

- **Notation maps** — Notation maps (also known as 'mind maps') are a powerful way to take notes, to represent ideas or to recap learning. Research by Robert Ornstein and Tony Buzan (amongst others) shows that not only are they fun, visual and yet logical way of showing the various strands that make up a topic, they are also very effective. Unlike traditional linear note-taking, notation maps are started at the centre of the page. Ideas then branch out from the central premise or topic, with related thoughts and facts tied in where relevant.

Example 1: Notation map
(Lewthwaite & Miscandlon, 2012)

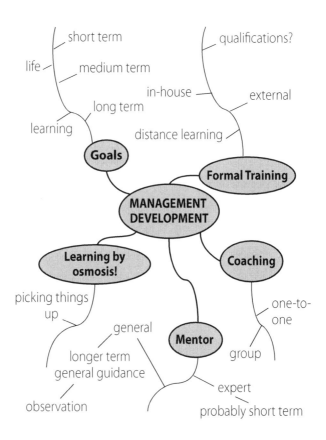

Example 2: Notation map (mind map) adopted from University of Bedfordshire Breo

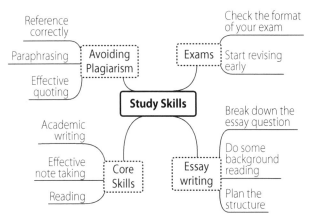

Devices like these are so effective because they appeal to both sides of the brain: they are linked and logical to keep your left brain happy and yet clever and colourful, to appeal to your right brain. We use our brains to best effect when we can satisfy both hemispheres.

Patricia Ikiriko's techniques of studying

This study technique encompasses breaking down large topics into smaller, more manageable segments. It differs from other techniques of studying in that it recognises that in addition to having the right approach to studying; students' comprehension is best assisted by noting key words for easy retention and remembering.

Main objectives of studying

The goals of academic pursuit are:

- to improve your competency in a particular area of study;

- to enhance your personal, cognitive and social development;

- to develop self-awareness;

- to critically understand the substantive content of a subject;

- to read and communicate effectively; and,

- to attain academic success in order to achieve a better quality of life.

As a student, you need to be aware of what is most important in studying, namely, developing an interest in, if not a passion for, the study materials, and planning for effective time management. It is also helpful for you to set your sights on a particular grade in order to achieve your set objectives. You might also keep in mind the professional qualification you would like to attain or the occupational field in which you would like to work. This will help you to discover the purpose and relevance of what is being studied.

Purpose of BREAKS

BREAKS is a study method developed by Patricia Ikiriko. Captured by the acronym BREAKS, the method involves:

Breaking down information into forms which are:

Readable;

Easy;

Achievable;

Knowable; and,

Structured.

It is proposed that this method assists the process of organising knowledge, including the acquisition of new information and organisation of different subject matters. Its purpose is to facilitate effective reading and concentration as well as an improved rate of assimilation of important material within a study topic. Furthermore, it can be used as a learning drill to aid memorisation and retention of information.

The BREAKS technique has the potential to help you to:

• investigate and analyse a subject in detail;

• increase your knowledge and retention of this knowledge;

- critically analyse and interpret complex information;

- select the relevant learning style and method suitable for studying;

- develop a sense of direction and purpose; and,

- assess your ability or understanding of a topic or theme.

Method related to learning style

The concept of BREAKS refers to a process of learning designed to enable you to improve your 'grip' on the materials under study and work effectively towards achieving the main objectives of studying, as outlined above. It is proposed that the most effective way for a student to make progress is by being actively involved with the material. This can be by visual, auditory or kinaesthetic/tactile means.

Significance and distinguishing characteristics of the BREAKS method

A variety of study techniques based on different modalities exist, as depicted in the table below (Cottrell, 1999; Marzano, 2004; Riding & Rayner, 1998).

Modality on which study method is based	Technique for learning
Memorisation	rehearsal and rote learning
Communication skills	reading and listening
Cues	flashcard training
Condensing information	summarising and using of keywords
Exam strategies	acronyms and mnemonics
Time management, organisation and lifestyle changes	tables, schedules, indexes
Visual imagery	drawings, spider diagrams

However, these study methods in the literature fail to address the psychological factors which affect students' behaviour. The BREAKS technique is unique because it addresses a wide scope of issues confronting students which can inhibit their academic performance. It is not just study techniques that can affect students' results, but also hidden psychological factors that must be identified in order to alter cognitions. Most students in the bottom eighty per cent make no effort to improve their skills, memory, and academic performance. They tend not to improve because of their on-going lack of interest in the subject, their poor productivity, and their nonchalant attitude towards their studies.

In contrast, many top-performing students take the trouble to go through their lecture notes and the recommended readings after each lecture. BREAKS represents a constructive method that you can use as a student to build up your motivation and interest in the subject matter.

Theoretical underpinning

The BREAKS method is aligned with a humanistic approach to education. Within the humanist tradition, Kirshenbaum and Henderson (1989) developed the theory of facilitative learning. The basic premise of facilitation theory is that learning will occur as a result of the educator acting as a facilitator and establishing an atmosphere in which learners feel comfortable with considering new ideas and are not threatened by external factors (Laird, 1985). This study technique can help you as a learner to increase your familiarity with the key concepts comprising any particular topic, and thereby feel less threatened by new concepts.

Scope

It is not possible for students to study with no methods; using the BREAKS technique can help you to break down a topic into more manageable segments, engage with each concept, and retain the content for use in exams and for enhancing your education. The technique may necessitate a re-organisation or modification of your current methods of studying, summarised in the table above, for 'taking in' what is being studied and retaining the basic ideas. It is a relatively simple way of learning to master new information in that the procedure can be learnt within a short period of time and can be applied to all educational fields, including the natural sciences, social sciences, humanities, music, technology, engineering, medicine, business and law. It is useful for learning throughout one's life. Each step in this method will now be described in detail.

The BREAKS procedure

B — Break down

R — Read

E — Easy

A — Achievable

K — Knowledge

S — Structure

Break down: Carefully deconstruct large topics into smaller pieces that can be read and absorbed one at a time. When a large amount of work is set for a single sitting, it tends to be demotivating and overwhelming, resulting in a loss of concentration and focus.

First, you should get an overview of the topic by looking at a lecture outline, or an index in a book, or even by 'Googling' the topic online. Be careful of using content from Wikipedia in your essays and projects; for many universities this is not an acceptable source or reference, and you are encouraged to use published books and peer-reviewed journal articles instead. For overview purposes, however, I cannot see any harm in using Wikipedia. Breaking down the material into smaller segments will help you to make the topic more manageable. Seeing on a single page, for example, how many concepts are required to adequately understand a topic, and how the various concepts within a topic fit together will help to make the learning ahead seem less daunting.

Readable: Ensure that you read at a rate that aids rather than hinders your understanding. Often you will discover that any topic can be highly interesting once you start reading it — not initially with an exam in mind, but with a view to finding out more about the subject. Read the material carefully and more than once to achieve a sound comprehension. When you feel that you have attained some familiarity with the material, you can then turn your attention to reading effectively. Reading effectively refers to the amount of material covered and the time taken to cover it. Monitoring the number of sub-topics you are covering within a larger topic (as per the index in step one above), as well as the time you take to cover them, will help to gauge whether you need to speed up your reading or note-taking or are on target.

Easy: This step will help you to keep sight of your studies in the midst of your daily activities. It involves arranging the topic of study in ways that are clear and legible, putting all your ideas in writing — whether on A4 sheets of paper, in a notebook, on a poster, or on flashcards. Wherever possible, try to find familiar examples relating to each concept in order to remember them more easily. These can be noted or drawn on the page in different colours, beneath a heading of the concept, thereby making the material more accessible. Set easy targets initially in order to accomplish your work according to your devised time schedule, discussed next, as this will foster a sense of progress and achievement.

Achievable: A study schedule should be drawn up showing the topics that need to be covered and when you plan to cover each one. These topics can be obtained from a lecture or syllabus outline or from an index in a textbook. Setting yourself the goal of studying four broad topics per day is unrealistic; it is preferable to develop a programme that will enable you to keep you working consistently towards your set goals at a steady pace.

Knowledge: Aim to enhance your knowledge of your own particular style of learning.

For those with a more visual style of learning, doing a structural drawing of the material may be most beneficial. For those who tend to take in information by auditory means, it may be useful to read the material into a MP3 Player and then play it back. For those who prefer learning by experiencing stimuli, the most beneficial techniques may entail integrating the key words of a topic into a song, or making memorable associations with 'emotionally-laden' words which the learner can easily remember. However, it could be helpful for all students to process the material by converting it into a lexical or numerical format such as noting down vocabulary, historical dates, or formulae on cards or posters. Your diagrams can illustrate points outlining your own understanding and incorporate various formats such as graphs, tables, charts and labels.

Thus, regardless of your learning style, a technique of note-taking, using keywords and other visual markings to organise the material, would be beneficial. Ensure that you find out any abbreviations before, during, and after lectures as these can facilitate the note-taking process. The more familiar you become with the keywords and main components of a topic, the more easily you will understand the topic (Brent, 2004).

Structure: Write out the basic points of your study material in a structured format. This can be in the form of a graph, map, table, bubbles, intersecting circles, rings, bands, spider diagram, or any visual marking that will help you make sense of what you have read on the topic. This process of documenting the vital points as you read will aid recall of what is studied as well as assist you in remaining focused and avoiding distractions. Moreover, organising the material in a visual format will foster engagement with the subject matter.

Example of BREAKS

Topic to be studied: Photosynthesis

This is a process that plants use in making their food by converting the chemical carbon dioxide into organic compounds, especially sugars, using the energy from sunlight. Photosynthesis uses carbon dioxide and water, releasing oxygen as a waste product.

• Step 1: List the key words

P — Photosynthesis

P — Plant

S — Sunlight

F — Food

Making these key words into a song could be especially beneficial for auditory learners.

- Step 2: Structure the key words in a diagram

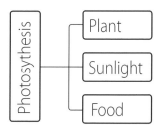

This simple diagram illustrates the process by which a plant makes its food through the conversion of energy from sunlight. For visual learners, it could be further enhanced by illustrating each word with a drawing and arrows to indicate the movement of energy.

Exercise

Practise using the BREAKS technique when studying. When structuring information for recall, bear in mind your preferred learning style, whether visual, auditory or kinaesthetic, and aim to design something that will play to your strengths.

Follow the best learning techniques suitable for you + Practise to attain academic excellence.

Chapter 7: The best way to read a book

Reading is something we usually begin to learn to do when we are in primary school. To be read to is, for most children, one of the biggest treats. To be able to read for oneself is a gift that can bring education and entertainment, knowledge, understanding and pleasure.

As you embark on your studies, you will be faced with a great deal of reading material. Each course has its own recommended reading and lecturers are likely to recommend that you read certain textbooks or articles to supplement what you have been taught. Add to that the subjects that you have a particular interest in and wish to explore in more depth for your own satisfaction, and it is clear that keeping up to date with the required reading is likely to take a good deal of your time.

That being the case, it makes sense to ensure that when you do read, you do it in a way that maximises your learning potential.

As a student, active preparation, organisation, reflection and rehearsal when reading are critical. Reading a piece of work is most effective when you survey the work first and create a road map or outline of the text, followed by reading the text in more detail to improve and elaborate the original outline.

When you read in order to learn, it is not enough to simply scan through the text, turning the pages as quickly as possible so that you can get to the end of one book and immediately pick up another. If we do not take a strategic approach to reading, then we might as well not bother at all.

What we need to be able to do is to read both quickly and effectively. We need to be swift due to the volume of reading we face, but we need to understand and assimilate the information we read and, equally importantly, we need to retain it.

The problem with reading without also using visual or auditory aids is the issue of memory loss. If we spend an hour learning something, then we will experience an increase in our ability to recall that information, but that increase will almost immediately begin to decline. After twenty-four hours, as much as eighty per cent of the detail in the information we learned will have been lost. To help you retain as much content as possible, it is helpful to use the BREAKS method described in Chapter 6.

Understanding the information we read

There's little point in reading at all if we don't make sure that we fully understand the meaning inherent in the words. When we start to study a new subject, we are likely to begin to come across new words and phrases specific to that subject; these will take time for us to get used to. In addition, we are now studying at a higher level and so can expect that the texts we study will be written in more complex language.

Consequently one of the first things we need to do is to make sure that we have a dictionary to hand when we read, either a traditional hardcopy dictionary or an online one. As soon as you come across an unfamiliar word, look it up and make a note of it. If you are studying a subject that has a lot of associated jargon, either seek out a glossary of terms or start to compile your own for easy reference. Do not move on with your reading until you are confident that you understand the meaning of the words on the page. (According to Adler's method, on which there is more information below, this task is not necessary for all levels of reading.)

Different levels of reading

Depending on what we wish to gain from reading material, we can approach the task in different ways. When you know what you want, you can decide how to read. We are going to look now at five different levels of reading, namely:

- Previewing.
- Elementary reading.

- Inspectional reading.

- Analytical reading.

- Syntopical reading.

Each has its place in your method of study. Let's take a closer look and examine how they fit together and can help you to learn more effectively.

Previewing

Previewing is useful when you are researching a subject. Consciously previewing books in order to assess their usefulness to you will ensure that you only spend additional time on those that will further your understanding of a subject.

To preview, first read the information on the back cover, then look at the table of contents. Finally, quickly skim the first couple of pages (or the first couple of pages of the most appropriate chapter, identified from the table of contents). As you take in the information, keep the following questions in mind:

- Is the book up to date?

- Is the content relevant to the research I am conducting?

- Does the author provide fresh insights into the subject?

If the answer to two or more of those questions is no, then you should look for another book. If the answer to two or more questions is yes, keep that book. You can then decide which type(s) of reading you should apply to it from the following options.

In *How to Read a Book* by Adler and Doren (1972) four levels of reading are distinguished: elementary; inspectional; analytical; and syntopical. It is those that we are going to look at now, beginning with elementary reading.

Elementary reading

Elementary reading describes the type of reading we are generally taught at school. It is concerned with recognising and understanding the words on the page, although not necessarily with looking for a deeper understanding than that. However, you must be able to read at an elementary level if you are to move on to the next level of reading.

Inspectional reading

Inspectional reading is intended to give the reader an overall understanding of a book. This is because if you know 'the lay of the land' before you begin reading in more depth, you will get more from the experience. Think of it as studying a map before you set out on a journey; if you have a rough idea of how you will get to your destination, then each step along the route will seem somewhat familiar.

Inspectional reading has two stages. Adler called the first stage 'systematic skimming' or 'pre-reading'. It consists of six steps:

- Look at the title page and, if the book has one, its preface.

- Study the table of contents.

- Check the index.

- Read the publisher's blurb.

- Look at the chapters that seem to be pivotal to its argument.

- Turn the pages, dipping in here and there, reading a paragraph or two, sometimes several pages in sequence, never more than that.

You will recognise some of the steps as those recommended in 'previewing' a book; inspectional reading, however, takes things a stage further. You undertake inspectional reading for books that have passed the questioning test at the preview stage. Stage one will allow you to assess the book's suitability and gain an understanding of its structure, contents and style, which will in turn indicate whether you should read the book in more detail or not. If you decide you should, then you move on to stage two of inspectional reading.

Adler termed the second stage of inspectional reading 'superficial reading'. He recommended that you should read through a book quickly and without attempting to understand every little term or concept. He insisted that you should not stop to look up things that you do not understand, but should simply move on, as the aim is to gain an overview of the book, to see the big picture rather than get bogged down in the minutiae. Adler asserts that this is especially important when reading large and difficult books, the danger being that if you try to understand everything before moving on, you will never finish reading the book.

Analytical reading

Having read a book inspectionally, you should (if necessary) move on to read it analytically. To this end, Adler gives us three stages, each with its own set of rules to follow, when doing this.

The first stage takes a structural approach and has four rules for finding out what a book is about:

1. Classify the book according to kind and subject matter.

2. State what the whole book is about with the utmost brevity.

3. Enumerate its major parts in their order and relation, and outline these parts as you have outlined the whole.

4. Define the problem or problems the author is trying to solve.

The second stage takes an interpretive approach and has four rules for interpreting a book's contents:

1. Come to terms with the author by interpreting his key words.

2. Grasp the author's leading propositions by dealing with his most important sentences.

3. Know the author's arguments, by finding them in, or constructing them out of, sequences of sentences.

4. Determine which of the stated problems the author has solved, and which he or she has not; as to the latter, decide which the author knew he or she had failed to solve.

The third stage, critiquing book as a communication of knowledge, has the following rules which fall under two headings:

A. General maxims of intellectual etiquette

1. Do not begin critiquing until you have completed your outline and interpretation of the book. (Do not say you agree, disagree, or suspend judgment until you can say 'I understand'.)

2. Do not disagree merely disputatiously or contentiously.

3. Demonstrate that you recognise the difference between knowledge and mere personal opinion by presenting good reasons for any critical judgments you make.

B. Special criteria for points of criticism

1. Show wherein the author is uninformed.

2. Show wherein the author is misinformed.

3. Show wherein the author is illogical.

4. Show wherein the author's analysis or account is incomplete.

Adler asserts that even though there are three stages to analytical reading, there is no requirement to read the book three times. Practise will be required, but it ought to be possible to attend to the requirements of each stage during a single intensive and active reading of the book.

Syntopical reading

Analytical reading is concerned with the in-depth study of an individual work, whereas syntopical reading requires you to read widely around a particular topic or concept. Syntopical reading will not necessarily require you to read a number of entire texts analytically; having identified several that deal with the topic you are researching or studying, you will only be required to read those chapters that deal directly with that topic. This enables you to compare the viewpoints and assertions of different authors and to arrive at your own interpretation of the data through your understanding and evaluation of their individual arguments.

Aiming to retain the information we read

As you read, you will want to make notes. If you are reading something that you own, then do not be afraid to underline or highlight certain words and phrases or key references. Make notes in the margin, dog-ear pages, bookmark with sticky notes or whatever helps you to best find what you are looking for when you return to a text.

This may take a bit of getting used to doing; after all, most of us have been told for years to take good care of our things and not to mark the pages of books. However, the books and papers we are talking about here are learning tools, and it is permissible and sensible to use these tools to our advantage.

When it is absolutely not acceptable to treat a book like that, however, is when it is someone else's book that we have borrowed; this includes library books. If you are working with borrowed books, copy things out rather than underlining or highlighting them or using sticky notes. What you do with your property is your business, but you must respect other people's property. If you have ever tried to study from a book that is covered in another student's markings, you will appreciate even more the need for this respectful approach!

Notation maps

We're shortly going to be looking at how you can read much more quickly than you currently do, but first I want to take a moment to discuss something that will mean it takes you longer to complete reading a book. The benefit, however, is that you will be able to refresh your memory as to what is in each individual chapter quickly and easily.

Earlier, in Chapter 6 'Developing the right study method for you', we looked at notation maps. Notation maps, as you may recall, are a terrific way to make notes and to show the links between different pieces of information. What I am going to suggest you do is this: when you finish reading a chapter of a book, while the information is still fresh in your mind, draw a notation map for that chapter. Pull out the key points and show how concepts and theories link up. It will take you a little time to do this, especially at first when you are new to making notation maps, but imagine being able to revise the contents of a book with twenty chapters simply by looking at just twenty pieces of paper. (If it helps you to make a notation map to give an overview of the contents of the entire book when you have finished reading, then by all means do that too.) Having these maps at your fingertips will allow you to refresh your learning easily and quickly, and will be invaluable when you are revising for exams.

Another useful thing to note down as you read are any quotes you may wish to use, plus the relevant references (see Chapter 8 'Good guide to different referencing styles'). In this way, if you want to refer to someone's work in your own academic writing (and you will), it is easy for you to identify and cite the source.

Reading more quickly

The last thing we are going to consider is how you can speed up the pace at which you read, while still taking in the information on the page. You may have been told for many years to read slowly and carefully to make sure that you do not miss anything. What would be more useful now, however, would be to learn to read quickly and mindfully — in other words, to learn to speed read.

Speed reading is an accepted technique and something that, with practise, anyone can master. The starting point is to measure the speed at which you currently read and then to take positive steps to increase that. You should be mindful of the fact that an increase in speed must not be at the expense of your level of comprehension.

There is a great deal of information available on speed reading, both in print and online, free and paid for. If this is something that interests you, the time it would take to practise should be paid back handsomely over the course of your studies, not to mention your lifetime.

Four vital points to remember

1. Before you read a book in detail, you should attempt to read the first and last paragraph as well as the abstract if available; these are usually summaries of the book.

2. Read the section headings if available and relate them to the outline given in the first and last paragraphs of the book.

3. If you find words in the abstract or opening/closing paragraphs that you do not understand, look them up using the glossary.

4. Scan the pages for summaries of the points you may need.

Exercise

Prepare, organise, and practise the techniques outlined here in order to get the most from your reading experiences.

Chapter 8: Good guide to different referencing styles

Academic writing involves presenting not only your own thoughts and ideas, but the thoughts and ideas of other people that you have studied, analysed and used to help you to form a cogent argument or arrive at a considered judgement. In any academic writing, whenever you mention or refer to someone else's idea, whether directly or indirectly, you need to indicate the source.

We present others' thoughts and ideas either by paraphrasing (putting someone else's ideas into your own words) or by quoting (directly copying someone else's words). Whenever you paraphrase or quote from someone else's published material, you must add a reference to give the author credit for those thoughts and ideas.

The reasons for referencing quoted and paraphrased work include:

- It proves you have read widely on the subject in order to gain a good understanding.

- It shows the context against which your own thoughts and ideas are set.

- It allows readers and tutors to check your sources for themselves.

- Not to add a reference would be to leave your open to charges of plagiarism.

Plagiarism refers to taking another person's thoughts, work or ideas and passing them off as your own. A serious matter, it can damage both your credibility and reputation, and can result in your work being failed.

As an aside here, I would strongly recommend, as suggested above (in Chapter 7 'The best way to read a book') that you make note of your references as you read. It can be frustrating to have to try to find an original source if all you have to go on is a scribbled quote or a short set of notes about something. Far better to note the author, date, title and page number as you go along and save time and trouble later.

How to reference

There are a number of accepted referencing styles. The most commonly used include Harvard; Modern Language Association America (MLA); Modern Humanities Research Association (MHRA); and British Numeric.

As a general rule, references will either be included within the text in parentheses, as a footnote, or as a reference number leading to an endnote. How references appear depends upon the specific requirements of the referencing style in use.

The chances are that your university will have its own preferred style and will have made a style guide available, either as a downloadable or accessible online resource, and you should make it your business both to know how to access it and also to adhere firmly to the guidelines. To fail to do so could cost you marks and/or grades.

What should you reference?

Irrespective of the style to be used, pretty much the same things are required to be referenced. These include:

- Books, including individual chapters.
- Magazines, periodicals and/or journals.
- E-books and e-journals.
- Newspapers.
- Websites/webpages.
- CD-ROMs.
- Films/television programmes/YouTube.
- Emails/tweets.
- Government documents.
- Lectures and seminars

As well as adding a reference or footnote within the text at the point at which the material appears, it is prudent to also compile a bibliography or reference list for inclusion at the end of the document.

Where a work is referenced that has one or two authors, they should be named, but should there be three or more, it is generally acceptable to name the first author and then add '*et al*' to indicate others.

The Harvard system requires sources to be cited briefly, in brackets, within the text, rather than in footnotes or endnotes. A full list of references, in alphabetical order, is included at the end of the document.

This system is arguably less intrusive and interrupts the flow less than a footnote or endnote reference system such as MHRA or MLA.

Where do you put this reference?

References should be included in all assignments, essays, presentations, dissertations, portfolios, and posters. Each reference in your work should appear in the body of the text and in a reference list at the end of your work.

As mentioned above, referencing applies to quotations or when paraphrasing (putting another's words in your own words). When using direct quotations, put inverted commas or quote marks ("... ") and provide the relevant page number. It is not enough to just put a reference at the end of the paragraph; you need to let the reader know your original source from the beginning to the end. Whenever you are using quotations that are three or more lines long, this should be indented from the left margin.

At the end of each assignment, a full reference list including the details of all the references discussed, quoted or paraphrased, should be provided to guide your readers.

Examples of referencing styles

	Harvard	MLA	MHRA
Citation within the text (Wherever possible, place at the end of a sentence)	Author(s); year of publication; page number if a direct quote.	Author(s) page number; (no punctuation in between)	Insert a footnote in the text. Author(s); title; (place of publication: publisher, year), page number(s).
Book (one author)	Author; year of publication; title; edition; place of publication: publisher.	Author; title; edition; place of publication; publisher; year of publication; print.	Author; title; (place of publication: publisher, year), page number(s).
Book (up to three authors Harvard style; two authors MLA & MHRA)	Authors; year of publication; title; edition; place of publication: publisher.	Authors; title; edition; place of publication; publisher; year of publication; print.	Authors; title; (place of publication: publisher, year), page number(s).

Book (more than three authors Harvard style; more than two authors MLA & MHRA)	First named author et al; year of publication; title; edition; place of publication: publisher.	First named author et al; title; edition; place of publication; publisher; year of publication; print.	First named author et al; title; (place of publication: publisher, year), page number(s).
Chapter within a book	Author of chapter; year of publication; title of chapter; editor(s); book title; place of publication: publisher; page number(s).	Author of chapter; title of chapter; book title; editor(s); publisher and place of publication; year of publication; page number(s); print.	Author of chapter; 'title of chapter'; in book title; editor(s); (place of publication: publisher, year), page number(s).
Article in a printed journal	Author; year; title; journal; volume; issue; pages.	Author; title; journal; volume; year; pages; print.	Author; title; journal; volume; year; pages.
Article in a journal accessed online	Author; year; title; journal; volume; issue; pages; URL; date accessed.	Author; title; journal; volume; year; pages; online collection; web; date accessed.	Author; title; journal; volume; year; URL; date accessed; page or paragraph numbers (if available).

So the same book reference would appear in the different styles thus:

- **Harvard:** Wilson, S. B. (1994) Goal Setting. 1st ed. New York: Amacom.

- **MLA:** Wilson, Susan B. Goal Setting. New York: Amacom, 1994. Print.

- **MHRA:** Susan B. Wilson, Goal Setting (New York: Amacom, 1994), p. 201-202.

There is a great deal of material available online with regard to the specifics of referencing should the guide provided by your university not answer all your questions. Check out some links that should prove useful on line

Exercise

Obtain a copy of your college or university's referencing style guide. Read it and ensure you thoroughly understand it.

If anything is unclear, then you should either:

1. Conduct online research to clarify the issues; or,

2. Compile a list of questions to put to your tutor, to ensure that you have a full understanding of the requirements.

N.B. If you are unable to obtain clarity by following step 1, proceed to step 2.

**Get into the habit of organising your
references as you go along.**

Chapter 9: How to research and source material for academic writing

Academic writing is the systematic process of organising your information in an orderly manner. It is therefore important to think of how you will search for information to identify the source materials needed for your writing.

Why is research desirable?

When you write an essay or paper, you are presenting your own thoughts and opinions, based on the thoughts and opinions, research results, and proven facts presented by others before you. Consequently it is necessary to conduct research so that you are well informed and come across as being a credible source.

A measure of your credibility will come from evidence that you are widely read on the subject that you are writing about. Proof that you are well read is given, at least in part, by the sources you cite in the body of your argument. If you can show that you have looked at a topic from a number of angles and understand the points of different authors with different standpoints, then you demonstrate a thorough understanding. This understanding lends your own opinions and argument more weight, as they are based on established theories and/or facts.

Where can you find the information you seek when researching a topic?

There are a number of sources of information, including:

- The Internet.

- Newspapers.

- Popular magazines.

- Scholarly journals.

- Research papers.

- Books.

- Government documents.

Let's take a closer look at those.

The Internet

The Internet can be a good place to start if you aim to gain an overview of a subject. Word your search carefully so that you get the most relevant results. If the number of results is huge, you may wish to add words or rephrase your search criteria; if the number of results is quite small, you may wish to remove words or, again, rephrase your search string.

Some specialist websites may carry more weight than general sites. You may find that as a result of your online reading, you collect useful references that signpost you to more scholarly sources.

Newspapers

Newspapers can be a useful source of information, particularly if there have been recent and newsworthy advances in your field of study. Again, they may signpost you to more scholarly sources or alert you to more recent research in the field.

Popular magazines

Popular magazines may be considered in the same light as newspapers. Again, while it would not do to have only references from popular magazines (and/or newspapers and the Internet), a well-chosen , appropriate reference will certainly not harm your case.

Scholarly journals

Scholarly journals, of the type in which experts in their field are likely to seek to publish their research papers, can be a powerful source of information. Searchable databases of journals, archives and other collections exist. Some are free to use and others are subscription-based. A good starting point is the university library, where the staff will be well-equipped to advise or assist you in your search.

Books

Unless you are writing about a very new field or topic, the chances are that there have been several books already written about the subject of your study. As an added bonus, it is likely that the writers of those books also researched widely, and so may have added value in the text in the form of further sources to which they can signpost you.

Government documents

The Government publishes a wealth of research material and information that could prove enormously useful to you. A vast amount is available online and is free to access, although there are charges for some items, especially printed papers. Get into the habit of routinely searching to see if there is material available at local or national level that would be pertinent to your studies.

Signposting

Any of the sources listed above can, as well as being useful in and of themselves, add value by signposting you to other relevant sources of information. Signposting can be a key element of your research. It can lead you down avenues of research that you might otherwise have not considered, and widen your knowledge immensely in the process. You must beware, however, of being led off at an irrelevant, albeit interesting, tangent. By all means make a note to go back to such reading at a later date, but do not allow it to divert your current line of research. Stay within the boundaries of your subject matter.

Library services

Please do make use of library services. University libraries are full of valuable and regularly updated information and staffed by experts. Remember that as you study, your feet are treading a well-worn path and that while many things may be new to you, they are familiar territory for others. Utilise their expertise and you will have more time to spend on actually studying, rather than finding sources of material to study.

Exercise

Consider what would be the best regular sources of research for you. (We're considering general rather than specialist sources here.) Make a list of those places it would be appropriate to seek information, and in what order, and make this standard practice to kick-start your research each time you embark on a new topic.

Chapter 10: Academic success tips

The length of time you spend completing your studies and working towards your degree has already been committed. It will take the same number of years irrespective of how well you do (provided you do not do so badly that you are obliged to withdraw from your course). It makes sense, therefore, to give yourself the best possible chance of success. This section includes hints, tips and checklists to help you to focus on the success you desire and deserve.

Seven tips to help you excel

1. Prepare before the class

Every success starts with one, small step. Take responsibility for your academic progress by setting your goals and studying your course material several times a week, even if only for short periods at a time. Develop a habit of reading the lecture slides and assigned readings before the lecture. When you read these materials, use a highlighter and outline the text to understand the lecture better.

2. Always attend classes

Your teachers or tutors will not only impart knowledge, but also explain theories and methodologies, and answer your questions, both in class and one-to-one, to help you gain a deeper understanding. You will benefit from seminars and group discussions when you attend classes. A university is a society that emphasises the importance of communication and listening to other people's opinions and ideas. It is very important to share your own thoughts and ideas with other students during class discussions. You may be surprised by the number of fresh thoughts and ideas that come from fellow students. During class, if you have trouble understanding material in the course, ask questions to clarify. Learn to consult the materials cited by the readings or lecturers, in the library or in databases after class for further understanding.

3. Master the skill of making useful notes

Learn how to listen actively and take accurate, thorough notes. Review and, if necessary, rewrite your notes as soon as possible to ensure you understand all the information. This is a good method of retaining the information learned and keeping it fresh in your memory. Integrate the notes you make with the slides and assigned materials and search further on related topics to gain more knowledge. Expressing ideas, facts and theories in your own words is a good way of testing and demonstrating your knowledge and understanding of the subject.

4. Make use of the library

Read, because Readers become Leaders. Consult your library for journal articles since these are likely to be the major source of information for your assignments and projects. It is important to keep up to date with the resources and services that are available to you in your library. Your school library guide will serve as a pointer to some of the major information resources and services available. For subject-related resources, look at the subject guide and if you need help, seek assistance from your academic liaison librarian team.

5. Surround yourself with committed learners

If your existing friends are not helping you to succeed academically, you may need to make friends instead with students who like to study. Seek out those that can help you and share ideas **and** ask relevant questions to boost your knowledge and understanding. Find someone who always attends classes and who takes good notes, and sit down together once in a while to compare notes. (Even if you listen actively and always attend classes, you're bound to miss a point here and there, so this can help you both out.)

Brian Tracy once said, 'If you are really serious about being the best and moving to the top of your field, you cannot afford to spend your time with people who are going nowhere in their lives, no matter how nice they are. In this sense, you must be perfectly selfish with regard to yourself and your future ambitions. You must set high standards on your friends and associates and refuse to compromise.' During meetings, ask questions to help you comprehend the material and listen for clarifications given by your friends, this help greatly for recollection when revising for examination.

6. Ask for help if you need it

Do not be ashamed to ask for help in class or from your fellow students. If you're having problems, show your teacher your notes and ask for some guidance, or stop by your study skills centre and have someone go over your notes with you. Ask questions to help you understand the material and listen for clarifications and examples that are given by your friends that are not on the slides; note each point to be included in your own notes. Consult the materials cited by the readings or class and library databases.

7. Prepare for examinations

Ensure that you read all the questions before selecting the one(s) that you will answer. Work out a general outline of your answer before you start writing on the question, this will help you to present your ideas systematically. Show your understanding of the topic through the use of good examples. Before handing in your paper, make sure you read through your answer to check for errors, spelling, missing information, and grammar.

Following the above tips will most likely help you to become and remain a high-achieving student.

Summary

Once you've got the general idea of the topic and familiarised yourself with any specialised vocabulary, **read** through it carefully again more than once to retain important information. You should then try to **rephrase** or organise the material in your own words or using your own summary devices which can help you to remember the key points easily when writing your examinations. Capture the main concepts and theories in notation maps for easy **recall**; add examples with familiar ideas related to the topic. After studying, **revisit** your original notes to keep your memory fresh. Make a note of anything you do not understand and **ask** questions in class.

Redeeming time

The common denominator among successful people is the ability to use their time wisely by taking action. Seize every moment; make a decision for success today. Don't wait, don't procrastinate. Success is for the student who says "Yes" to success, who plans for it and reaches out for it. When you say "I will wake up from this time to that time, to study", you wake up. When you say "I'll read this book at this time", you read it. When you say "I'll go to school", you go. Make up your mind to be a success.

Time is fixed and there never seems to be enough of it. You therefore have to prioritise. If you have an assignment or project due, do it at the time stipulated for it. Successful students are time-conscious. Success is waiting for the student who makes decisions. Do not spend all your time watching television and DVDs and visiting social networking sites. The actors you are watching on TV and the innovators who created the social networking sites have put their best into their respective careers; don't allow them to detract from the time you could be spending achieving your best in your own chosen career.

Locus of control revisited

In Chapter 2, I discussed why it is important to develop an internal locus of control (LOC). Students who believe that the results of their examinations are due to their own effort and ability are said to have an internal LOC. In contrast, those who believe that their grades are caused by powerful others, bad luck, the test structure, or the faults of the teacher are said to have an external LOC.

A study I conducted in schools on 20 boys and 20 girls (aged 15-21) in Nigeria in 2012 found two distinct explanations for locus of control. Those with an internal LOC accepted responsibility when they failed in their studies, while those with an external LOC attributed their failure variously to the negative, discouraging attitudes of parents or guardians, peers, relatives and neighbours, as well as teachers' unsupportive attitudes and other forces beyond their control, such as a noisy environment.

Some participants in the study blamed themselves for not studying well and not understanding the concepts taught in the class. Many reported negative perceptions of themselves, concerning negative beliefs, negative self-appraisals and self-blaming attitudes that limited their ability to develop good study habits, such as reading, completing homework, and studying after a lecture.

Research has shown that one's self-concept plays a significant role in shaping one's behaviour (Sampson, 1981; Smith & Bond, 1993). Some participants expressed a fear of attempting to read and failing to understand the concepts being studied. For some, academic failure prompted a reflective process about their future ability to succeed academically. For others, poor performance was an immediate signal to give up. Some had developed a poor self-concept and expressed reluctance to try again. The following quotes from four participants reflect a negative self-concept:

It's because I don't take my studies serious. I don't read, I don't help myself, always go out to play, feel less concerned about my academic. I don't read and in the school I always play.

(Participant 2, boy, class year 10, age 18)

I don't read my books. I do not understand when the teacher is, is teaching.

(Participants 17, girl, class year 10, age 19)

I don't really do my work because I don't really copy my notes; I'm not that fast in writing so by the time I can finish, you know, they might have clean the board. And also I feel, since I'm not that fast now let me just give up.

(Participant 19, boy, class year10, age 20)

I'm always scared, I don't think I can do well because I don't understand whatever they're teaching me.

(Participant 14, girl, class year10, age 17)

This research showed that after counselling, students reported using more effective methods of studying and improving their attitudes, self-confidence and study habits. Awareness of their own and others' negative attitudes was the basis for this positive change in the LOC, that is, from external LOC to internal LOC.

You may not be able to change yesterday but you can plan today to change your tomorrow. To do something about your tomorrow, you have got to do it today. So make the most of your time.

I believe every person has the potential within to succeed. Every great achievement demands hard work. Success is not accidental, but comes about through the continual cultivation of sound habits, carefully worked-out goals, and diligence in adhering to an action plan (Ikiriko, 2010). It is never too difficult to achieve success if you try hard enough. You have all it takes to make it. Remember that no one can make it for you, but others can help you to build on what you have started. The keys to your success are commitment and hard work. You owe it to yourself to make the most of the opportunities available to you while you are at school, college or university. You have the potential to take a step to a brighter future.

Last words:

A case study: From failure to success

Amuzie, a first class honours in applied biology and who was also awarded the overall best graduating student/valedictorian, Rivers State University of Science and Technology, Port Harcourt, Nigeria (2004) below describes how an academic weak student can suddenly become a strong student to attain academic excellence. She introduces William F. Kumuyi pastor of the Deeper Life Bible who is a former university don and author of over 20 books who graduated with a First Class honours in Mathematics. I was not always a brilliant student, Kumuyi narrates in his own words

When I was very young, in my early school days, I failed a lot. It appeared that I could not pass any subjects at all. It was so pronounced that I lost interest in schooling but I just managed to push on. Most of the time, I was promoted on trial. Many of my teachers and fellow students felt that I could not do well at all. Things continued like this with me until I got to Form Four in Secondary School and **suddenly decided to make a change**.

I took a decision to succeed and prove people who think I can't make it wrong. I can't explain what motivated me to take this decision, I just decided to change.

That year, 1960, I passed my examinations to Class Five. In Class Five, **I set a goal of distinction** in all my subjects and **decided to work hard towards** it. **I asked questions in class, read, studied, did everything I should**. In fact, my classmates and teachers were surprised at the sudden change that came upon me.

At the end of my secondary education, I had one of the best results in my school, I moved on to university, and all through my years in the university I did well and graduated as the best student in my department that year.

Good luck, and enjoy the learning experience

About the author

Patricia Orlunwo Ikiriko is a trained counselor who has worked with different organizations involving young people for over 18 years. She is happily married to Hon. Hope Odhuluma Ikiriko and a mother blessed with two children Doxa and Chanan-Christie Ikiriko; two foster children Naomi Miriam and Timiadedike Seker and a granddaughter Sara-Louise Seker.

She holds a Graduate Diploma in Psychology from the University Of East London, a Master's degree in Education Guidance and Counselling from the University Of Port Harcourt Rivers State Nigeria, a B.Ed in Education and Guidance, Counselling and Psychology from University Of Ibadan Nigeria and a National Certificate in Education from the University Of Ibadan Nigeria.

She is a professional member of the British Psychology Society, the American Counselling Association, Counselling Association of Nigeria and a PhD student in Psychology at the University of Bedfordshire, UK.

She is involved in various youth and correction programmes at the Redeemed Christian Church of God - Chapel of Glory International (RCCG-CO-GI), a non-profit organisation in Watford, Hertfordshire.

Patricia has a passion in helping young people to discover their unique and hidden potential and encouraging them to fulfill their destiny in order to determine exactly who they are and what they want by setting clear, measurable, and achievable goals. She helps them to create a strategic plan as a sign-post to their desired destination, and develop confidence in themselves, along with the qualities of endurance, persistence and determination to remain focused to accomplish their dream.

Her inspiration was developed through her wealth of experience of working with young people in schools and different organisations for over 18 years. She is currently conducting a research on 'How to Develop Good Study Habits'.

In addition, she is working with academically underachieving students to investigate the attitudinal/psychological factors which result in poor academic performance.

She aims to recommend strategies to help people understand and develop effective approaches to studying. She recognises that the best medium for reaching young people and accomplishing these goals would be through book, a simple illustrative and accessible ways, which will convey key ideas and information to today's students.

References

Adair, J. (2011). *Lexicon of leadership: The definitive guide to leadership skills and knowledge.* UK: Kogan Page Limited.

Ajzen, I. (2001). Attitudes, personality, and behaviour (2nd Ed.). Milton-Keynes, England: Open University Press / McGraw- Hill.

Amuzie, C. (2008). Simple steps to academic excellence. Port Harcourt: Nova.

Asplund, C. L., Dux, P. E., Godwin, D., Martin, J. W., Marois, R. & Tombu, M. N. (2011). A unified attentional bottleneck in the human brain. Proceedings of the National Academy of Sciences of the United States of America, 108(33).

Baker, S. & Constantinidou, F. (2002). Stimulus modality and verbal learning performance in normal aging. *Brain and Language, 82(3),* 296–311.

Bloom, B. (1976). *Human characteristics and school learning.* New York: McGraw-Hill.

Bohner, G., & Wanke, M. (2002). *Attitudes and attitude change.* New York: Psychology Press.

Brent, D. (2004). *Inventions of teaching: A genealogy.* Mahwah, New Jersey: Lawrence Erlbaum.

Buzan, T. (1984). *Use your head: Innovative learning and thinking techniques to fulfil your mental potential.* British Broadcasting Corporation,

Buzan, T. (1996). *The mind map book: How to use radiant thinking to maximize your brain's untapped potential.* New York: Plume, Cottrell, S. (2003). *Teaching study skills and supporting learning.* Palgrave Study Guides. Palgrave: Macmillan.

Doob, L. W. (1947). The behaviour of attitudes. *Psychological Review, 54(3),* 135-156.

Eagly, A. H., & Chaiken, S. (1993). *The psychology of attitudes.* Belmont, CA: Thomson.

Gallagher, R. P, Golin, A., & Kelleher, K. (1992). The personal, career, and learning skills needs of college students. *Journal of College Student Development, 33(4),* 301-309.

Gantt, H. L. (1910). Work, wages and profit. *The Engineering Magazine.* New York.

Goertzel, T. G. & Hansen, A. M. W. (2004). Cradles of eminence (2nd Ed.). Childhood of more than 700 famous men and women. United States: Great Potential Press.

Harvard Referencing Style (APA) [Online]. Available: http://www.harvardgenerator.com/. (Accessed 11 November 2012).

Hembrooke, H. & Gay, G. (2003). The laptop and the lecture: The effects of multitasking in learning environments. Journal of Computing in Higher Education, 15

Honey, P. & Mumford, A. (2006). *The learning styles helper's guide.* Peter Honey Publication Limited. [Online]. Available: http://peterhoney.com/documents/ Learning-Styles-Helpers-Guide_QuickPeek.pdf. (Accessed 11 November 2012).

Ikiriko, P. O. (2010). *You can be richer than your parents.* London: Ecademy Press.

Jonassen, D. H. & Grabowski, B. L. (1993). *Handbook of individual difference, learning, and instruction.* Hillsdale, NJ: Lawrence Erlbaum.

Junco, R., & Cotten, S. R. (2012). No A 4 U: The relationship between multitasking and academic performance. Computers & Education, 59(2), 505–514.

Keefe, J. W. (1979). Learning style. An overview. In J. W. Keefe (Ed.). *Student learning styles: Diagnosing and prescribing programs.* Reston. V. A. National Association of Secondary School Principals (pp. 1-17).

Kirschenbaum, H., & Henderson, V. (Eds.). (1989). *The Carl Rogers Reader.* Boston: Houghton Mifflin.

Laird, D. (1985). *Approaches to training and development.* Mass: Addison-Wesley.

LaPiere, R. T. (1934). Attitudes versus actions. *Social Forces, 13*, 230-237.

Lewthwaite, J., & Miscandlon, S. (2012) Getting Things Done in Business. {Online}. Available: https://www.amazon.co.uk/dp/B008P4W9CA. (Accessed: 8 September 2012).

Lombardi, V. (1960). The Lombardi Era. In V. Lombardi (2001), *What It Takes to Be #1: Vince Lombardi on Leadership.* New York: McGraw-Hill.

Mandino, O. (1985). *The greatest salesman in the world.* Hollywood: Bantam.

Marzano, R. J. (2004). *Building background knowledge for academic achievement: What works in schools.* Alexandria, VA: Association for Supervision and Curriculum Development.

Mayer, R., & Moreno, R. (2003). Nine ways to reduce cognitive load in multimedia learning. Educational Psychologist, 38(1), 43–52.

Mind Map adopted from University of Bedfordshire [Online]. Available: http://breo.beds.ac.uk (Accessed: 4 September 2012).

Modern Language Association (MLA) [Online]. Available: http://www.mla.org/style (Accessed: 11 November, 2012).

Mortimer, J., Adler, M. J., & Doren, C. V. (1972). *How to read a book* (2nd Ed.). New York: Simon & Schuster.

O'Brien, L. (1989). Learning styles: Make the student aware. NASSP Bulletin October, 73, 85-89.

Ornstein, R. (1977). *The psychology of consciousness.* New York: Harcourt Brace Jovanovich.

Parkinson, C. N. (2010). *Trade in the Eastern seas 1793-1813.* Cambridge: Cambridge University Press.

Park, I.-S., Kim, N. (1998). Thiolated salmonella antibody immobilization onto the gold surface of piezoelectric quartz crystal. Biosens. *Bioelectron. 13,* 1091-1097.

Riding, R. & Rayner, S. (1998). *Cognitive styles and learning strategies: Understanding style differences in learning and behaviour.* London: Fulton Publishers.

Rosen, L. D., Lim, A. F., Carrier, L. M., & Cheever, N. A. (2011). An empirical examination of the educational impact of text message-induced task switching in the classroom: Educational implications and strategies to enhance learning. Psicologia Educativa, 17(2), 163–177.

Rotter, J. B. (1954). *Social learning and clinical psychology.* New York: Prentice-Hall.Sampson, E. E. (1981). Cognitive psychology as ideology. *American psychologist, 36,* 730-734.

Schraw, G., Wadkins, T., & Olafson, L. (2007). Doing the things we do: A grounded theory of academic procrastination. Journal of Educational Psychology, *99(1),* 12-25.

Semin, G. R. (1986). The individual, the social, and the social individual. *British Journal of Social Psychology, 25,* 177-180. Smith, P. B. & Bond, M. H. (1993). Social psychology across culture analysis and perspective. Hemel Hempstead Harvester Wheatsheaf.

Stewart, K. L., & Felicetti, L. A. (1992). Learning styles of marketing majors. *Educational Research Quarterly, 15(2),* 15-23.

The Modern Humanities Research Association (MHRA) [Online]. Available: http://www.mhra.org.uk (Accessed: 11 November, 2012).

The *Oxford English Dictionary* (*OED*), Oxford University Press [Online]. Available: http://en.wikipedia.org/wiki/Oxford_English_Dictionary (Accessed: 10 November, 2012).

Wood, E., Zivcakova, L., Gentile, P., Archer, K., De Pasquale, D., & Nosko, A. (2012). Examining the impact of off-task multi-tasking with technology on real-time classroom learning. Computers & Education, 58(1), 365–374.

43242605R00103

Made in the USA
Middletown, DE
04 May 2017